Everybody's GRAMMAR

Book 2

Mary Green

Bruce Martin

Liz Martin

James Sale

Keith Selby

Acknowledgements

Editor: Andrew Brown and Bob Munro   Layout artist: Patricia Hollingsworth
Illustrations: Anthony Maher, Jeremy Bays, Ian McGill – Graham-Cameron Illustration;
           Gary Clifford – The Drawing Room
Cover image: Digital Vision Ltd   Cover design: Kim Ashby, Ed Gallagher

© 1998 Folens Limited, on behalf of the authors.

British Library Cataloguing in Publication Data. A catalogue record for this book is available from the British Library.

First published 1998 by Folens Limited, Dunstable and Dublin.
Folens Limited, Albert House, Apex Business Centre, Boscombe Road, Dunstable, LU5 4RL, England.

ISBN 1 86202486–3

Printed in Singapore by Craft Print.

© Folens

Texts and sources

This is a book about various aspects of grammar, but it draws upon a wide range of sources – from poems and plays, through to novels and newspaper articles. As a result the publishers wish to thank the following:

Page 7   *Archy's Life of Mehitabel* by Don Marquis (Faber & Faber).

Page 9   *Odds and Ends* by Alistair Reid.

Page 14   *Tea for Two*. Words by Irving Caesar. Music by Vincent Youmans.
© 1920 Harms Inc, USA. Warner/Chappell Music Ltd,
London W6 8BS. Reproduced by permission of IMP Ltd.

Page 15   *Anthem for Doomed Youth* by Wilfred Owen.

Page 18   *I am a syllable* by David Orme.

Page 19   *As lightning flashes* by Matsuo Basho (Weatherhill Publishers).

Page 21   *In Watchful Community* by Thom Gunn (Faber & Faber).

Page 23   *The Lady of Shalott* by Alfred Lord Tennyson.

Page 26   *English Spelling Blues* inspired by *Hints On Pronunciation For Foreigners*.

Page 32   *Suicide in the Trenches* by Siegfried Sassoon (Faber & Faber).

Page 32   *Sea Timeless Song* by Grace Nichols (Virago).

Page 62   *Who's There* and *The Forgotten Enemy*, by Arthur C Clarke. Printed in
Of Time and Stars (Puffin).

Page 68   *The Secret Diary of Adrian Mole Aged 13 $\frac{3}{4}$* by Sue Townsend
(Methuen).

Page 68   *Kilvert's Diary* edited by William Plomer (Penguin).

Page 68   *Anne Frank – The Diary of A Young Girl, 1942–1944* The Definitive
Edition (Penguin).

Page 76   *Yesterday* by John Lennon and Paul McCartney (Music Sales).

Page 78   from *Found Poem* by Michael Benedikt.

Page 79   'Activities Week' illustration based on work by Simon Atkinson.

Page 80   *Berlin Wall* by Martin Kerry. Thanks to Peter Green.

Page 84   from *Vegan Delight* by Benjamin Zephaniah.

Page 85   *Syrup Prunes* recipe by J Partridge in *The Treasurie of Commodious
Conceites and Hidden Secrets*.

Introduction

Folens' *Everybody's Grammar* is a comprehensive course for pupils between the ages of 11–14, and aims to make language skills and usage as accessible and lively as possible. 'Grammar' here is taken to include a wide-range of definitions and ideas; at its most basic, it is the heart of language – the letter – which can denote both sound and symbol (and this is where all three books start). At its most expansive, it denotes the whole system of language – the holistic text – of which letter, sound, phrase, sentence and so on are constituent parts. For this reason, there are poems, prose and script extracts, studies of genre and extended writing activities to run alongside the individual elements that make up the whole.

In addition, the books provide practical and helpful sections designed to aid the teacher in developing the pupil's skills and understanding.
There are:

- *regular reviews of skills covered previously*
- *tests and exercises*
- *longer assignments requiring pupils to practise what they have learned*
- *helpful menus of targets so that pupils can set realistic goals.*

Each book begins with a section called 'Starting points' which enables pupils to review where they are with regard to language knowledge and usage. In Book 2, pupils are tested on basic punctuation, parts of speech, spellings and so on, before they move into the main body of the text.

The books then broadly follow a framework of:

- *word level work*
- *sentence level work*
- *whole text level work.*

It is not the intention of the authors that this should be a straitjacket, it is merely a useful way of providing a sense of how language consists of a series of interlocking parts.Work on paragraphs, for example, appears in 'Shaping texts' but, equally, it could appear in 'Other labels '.

In essence, the books are based on the notion that this is a 'grammar' that teachers will recognise – made up of those labels children ought to know to enable them to use language more effectively and imaginatively – and also consisting of opportunities to explore language areas that have been perhaps neglected in recent years.

Contents

Page

Punctuation

> *The tasks and exercises in this section are ways for you to review what you already know about certain aspects of English language and grammar.*

Tasks

 The following need either a question mark or an exclamation mark. Write them out correctly.

It won't matter will it

Watch out

Do you think we should take the risk

I can't believe it

Five, four, three, two, one. Go

 Write a short paragraph that contains one of the above, using question marks and exclamation marks.

 Rewrite the short extract below, putting in capital letters, full-stops, commas and a question mark:

> Some towns began as small communities hundreds of years ago and the name of a place can tell us about its origin in the past people chose sites where they could find water food and shelter ford for example is an old english name meaning river crossing can you guess what the name oxford means

Sometimes writers leave out punctuation because they want to express an idea in an unusual way.

Read the following. It is part of a long poem narrated by a cockroach called Archy.

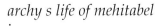
archy s life of mehitabel
i
the life of mehitabel the cat

boss i am engaged on a literary
work of some importance it is
nothing more nor less
than the life story of
mehitabel the cat she is
dictating it a word
at a time and all
the bunch gather around to listen but
i am rewriting it as i go along
boss i wish we
could do something
for mehitabel she is

Don Marquis

How does the lack of punctuation make you read this poem?
Describe in a paragraph the kind of impression the poet creates about Archy and Mehitabel.

 Choose one of these ideas:

– meeting your double
– seeing a ghost
– testing your own flying machine
– turning into a frog
– remembering a nightmare.

Use the idea to write a letter to a friend. Use full-stops, capital letters, commas, question marks, exclamation marks and apostrophes. Then use the same idea in a poem to the same friend without using punctuation.

When you have finished ask a partner to proof-read your letter. Then compare your letter and poem by noting at least five differences between them.

Parts of speech

> 'Parts of speech' is the term we give to the names of certain words. Check how well you know them.

Tasks

 Draw a table like this:

Parts of Speech	Verb	Common noun	Pronoun	Proper noun	Adjective	Adverb
Definition	expresses action					
Examples	scream					

Write the following in the proper places on your table:

- describes a noun or pronoun
- describes a verb
- takes the place of a noun
- the name of something
- special names.

school	he	Meena	loudly	it	sting
we	mouse	carefully	tiny	she	suddenly
Errol	think	dog	Sue	moody	laugh
bark	wasp	yesterday	squeak	harmless	foolish

 Two words have come together to form compound nouns in the lists below. Write them out and underline:

- the parts that are **verbs** in red
- the parts that are **nouns** in blue
- the parts that are **adjectives** in green.

diving-board	green-card	swimsuit
haircut	playground	blackboard
Sunday	jamjar	railway
bookshelf	blue-jeans	suitcase

Collective nouns

 Discuss briefly with a partner what the term 'collective nouns' means.

 Read below from *Odds and Ends* by Alistair Reid. He has made up his own collective nouns.

> A grumbling of buses
> A humbug of packages
> A gundulum of garbage cans
> A scribbitch of papers
> A snigglement of string
> A tribulation of children.

Write down what you think each one means. (For example, is 'humbug' a large pile of sticky packages?) Check in a dictionary.

Write a short paragraph saying why you think Alistair Reid chose them.

 Copy out the table below and match the following. The first has been done for you.

A litter of ——→ pups
A gang of   friends
A bunch of   musicians
A pack of   angels
A band of   singers
A choir of   thieves
A flock of   grapes
A host of   wolves

Now make up your own special collective nouns for the following:

jamjars   **rattlesnakes**   **computers**   **T-shirts**   **footballers**

blue-jeans   **street-lights**   **butterflies**   **dinosaurs**   **caravans**

Tenses

> You may remember that verbs are spoken or written so that the action takes place in the:
>
> Past (time or tense) – 'she danced'
> Present – 'she dances'
> Future – 'she will dance'
>
> There can also be differences within a tense. Both of the following are in the present tense:
>
> She dances.   She is dancing.

Tasks

 Which example ('dances' or 'is dancing') suggests that it is being carried out as you read it and which suggests that it happens regularly?

 Copy out this table and finish ticking the correct boxes. Some ticks have been included. Correct them if they are wrong.

	Past	Present	Future
They are ...	✔		
They have gone ...			✔
He speaks ...			
She went ...			
It is barking ...		✔	
They will be glad ...			
She swam ...			
We will say ...			

Choose one of the listed tenses and use it in a short paragraph. Then rewrite the paragraph in a different tense.

 Writers change tenses to create different moods but it is easy to change tenses without meaning to.

Read the following passage:

New York was the first city she visited and for weeks after leaving she wakes up in the night with the sound of sirens wailing in her ears. It was a high-pitched shriek of distress and it never fails to startle and frighten her. The whole city seems to be screaming out for help.

Notice which words are written in different tenses. Rewrite the passage so that the tenses make sense.

Inverted commas

Inverted commas (speech marks) are used, as you may recall, to show when someone is speaking.
"Have you brought your new bike, today?" he asked.
The words inside the inverted commas are the actual words spoken.

Tasks

 The following passage has been laid out correctly, but there are no inverted commas. Write it out correctly.

My older sister walked towards me with a look of determination.
    You're gonna get it now! she screeched.
My heart was beating and I could feel the sweat breaking out above my lip.
She grabbed my collar.
    You miserable little ... , she began.
Suddenly, the door swung open.
    What do you think you're up to, Rosie? announced David, my older brother.
A great feeling of relief swept over me and I felt strong again.
    Let go of me! Let go of me! I shouted and ran out of my room.

 Now write the beginning of the story. Use dialogue and inverted commas.

Spelling, prefixes and suffixes

Check your knowledge by completing the three tasks below.

Tasks

 Use the prefix table to write down as many words as you can.

	de	re	con
ex	press	claim	tent
pre	serve	view	sent
in	crease	form	tact

List any words that you don't know the meaning of and check them in a dictionary. Think of three more words that have prefixes.

 Look at the words below. Write down as many new words as you can adding the suffixes from the box.

king	excite	agree
advertise	read	kind
mean	like	free

Suffixes	
ness	dom
able	ment

Words can change when you add a suffix.
Write out the new word correctly.

beauty + ful =   supply + ed =

early + est =   empty + er =

carry + age =   merry + ment =

easy + ly =   happy + ness =

 We often confuse the spelling of words that have 'ie' or 'ei' in them. Copy and complete the following diary entry correctly, check your answers in a dictionary and record any mistakes.

Friday October 31st.

Rec__ved a strange parcel today. It had three for__gn stamps on it and w__ghed a ton. When I opened it I couldn't bel__ve my eyes! __ght crystals twinkled up at me and a card with a br__f message read, 'A present for you'.
Who has sent this? I wondered. Is someone up to misch__f?

Proof-reading

Using proof-reading signs is a way of highlighting things that need correcting.
See how well you can use them to help redraft the newspaper report correctly.

Tasks

 Rewrite the news report below using the signs to guide you.

spelling mistake

new paragraph

capital letter

unclear, rewrite

punctuation mistake

new sentence

full-stop

add more

Rough Ride For Rowdies

Slinger's transport Company are to ban local pupils from using there buses and the ban will last three weeks a spokesperson for Slinger's said that the company took the desision with regret. He added that in the face of mounting conplaints from residents concerning threatening behaviour the company had no choice Selected buses will not run between 3.30 and 4.30 during weekdays. Pupils and their parents are up in arms and feel the ban is unjustified. One irate mother claimed that slinger's hadn't consulted them and rowdiness is caused by only a few. Slinger's are using a sledge-hammer to crack a nut , she said.

governors and headteachers of the two scholls involved expressed concern about pupils' welfare particularly yonger ones who live some distance away.

---

② Write a letter to the newspaper from a pupil disagreeing with Slinger's decision.
Set your letter out clearly and use appropriate punctuation.

Alliteration

> When writers use language they often put together words that begin with the same sound because it helps make the writing memorable and reinforces the meaning. This is alliteration. For example: <u>s</u>oftly <u>s</u>inging.

Read the following:

a) **Tea for two**
   And two for tea
   Me for you
   And you for me ...

b) **Kung Fu Kenny Kicks Off**

c) **Every dog has its day**

d) **The wild winds weep,**
   **   And the night is a-cold;**
   Come hither, Sleep,
   **   And my griefs unfold:**

e) **Peter Piper picked a peck of pickled pepper.**
   A peck of pickled pepper Peter Piper picked.

f) **Take time out with Tonkins Travel.**

Tasks

 In pairs, discuss what types of language the above examples come from and what alliteration is used. Then write out the list below and complete the grid.
(The first has been done for you.)

Type of writing	Example	Alliteration
tongue-twister	e	on letter 'p'
advertisement		
newspaper headline		
poem		
saying		
song		

 Also in pairs, write out an advertising jingle to launch one of the products below. Use alliteration and draw a suitable picture to go alongside it.

banana toothpaste	**vegetarian pet food**	**a mini-motorbike**
a spinach face-pack	**a foldaway schoolbag**	**chocolate soup**

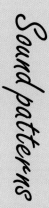

 3 Read this poem to yourself:

For Swallows
Sudden swallows swiftly skimming,
Sunset's slowly spreading shade,
Silvery songsters sweetly singing,
Summer's soothing serenade.

Anon

 4 Write down what you think the poem is about.
Make brief notes on how it makes you feel – sad, happy, relaxed, wistful?
Note down what the alliteration is and how it adds to the meaning.

Copy out the table below. Add more words beginning with the same sound to each column. Choose one list and use the words to help you write a poem of four lines in the style of the one above.

b	f	s	l	m	w
blunder	firefly	serpent	laugh	meander	winter

5 Wilfred Owen used alliteration for a more serious purpose. Look at the start of his poem written from the trenches in the First World War shortly before he was killed:

> **What passing bells for those who die as cattle?**
> **– Only the monstrous anger of the guns.**
> **Only the stuttering rifles' rapid rattle**
> **Can patter out their hasty orisons ...**

from *Anthem for Doomed Youth*

Copy out the line that uses alliteration and write down why Owen chose to use alliteration. Note down any other clever uses of sound.

Further work

 6 Decide what the following headline means, work out a storyline and write a newspaper article about it. Use alliteration in the first few sentences.

YAHOO OVER YOB BOY

Onomatopoeia

> *Usually you cannot tell the meaning of a word from its sound. For instance, the sounds of the words 'man' and 'dog' do not tell us that one is a two-legged animal, the other four-legged, or even that they are both living things. But some words are connected to their sounds.*
>
> *The word 'buzz' suggests the noise of a bee. We call these connections between sound and meaning onomatopoeia.*

Read the following:

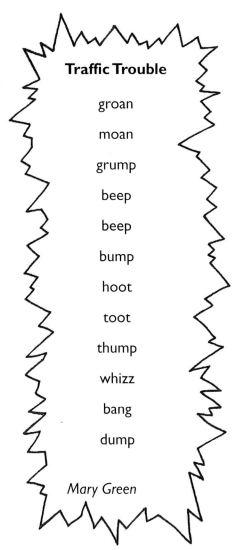

Traffic Trouble

groan

moan

grump

beep

beep

bump

hoot

toot

thump

whizz

bang

dump

Mary Green

Traffic Blights

red
amber
green
red stop
green go
amber in between so

red amber green
red stop green go
amber in between so

red amber green
blinking
red amber green blinking?
red amber go green
red amber no green
red spots
green stops
amber on the blink
what?
red go!
green stop!
red amber green blinking
re...am...gr...blinking traffic
rrr..arr..grr..blinking traffic lights!

Mary Green

Tasks

 With a partner, discuss what is happening in the poems above. How are they similar?

Are they both onomatopoeic poems? Explain your answer.

In *Traffic Blights* sight as well as sound is used. There are also double meanings (words with more than one meaning). Find an example of such a word and write it down. Then write down six other words that have double meanings.

 Decide if these words have a heavy, light or sharp sound. Copy the table and tick the correct boxes. Add more onomatopoeic words. Then choose from your list and write an onomatopoeic poem that is heavy, light or sharp. Give your poem a suitable title.

	heavy	light	sharp
crack			✔
thump			
swish			
tinkle			
thud			

 Think of a character such as Batman or Catwoman and plan a simple storyline (for example, Catwoman captured by an underground monster).
Draw your story in comic strip form.
Add onomatopoeic words (such as POW! AHH! SLURP!). Don't use ordinary sentences.
Leave the speech bubbles empty.
When you have finished ask a partner to fill in the speech bubbles to show how far they understand your story.

Further work

 Write onomatopoeic words to suit the following:

- screeching brakes
- wailing cats
- howling babies
- dripping water
- galloping horses
- birdsong

Choose one and turn it into a ten-line poem using what you have learned.

Syllable patterns

> You may remember that words are divided into single units of sound called 'syllables'. For example:
>
> 'swamp' has one syllable, 'riv/er' has two and 'croc/o/dile' has three.
>
> Some poets, such as rappers, emphasise this rhythm. Others arrange words so that they form special syllable patterns.

A **lantern** poem makes the shape of a lantern.

Light   (one syllable)
Breezy   (two syllables)
Kite flying
High and windy
Days

The poem *I am a syllable* makes the shape of a **pyramid**.

I
am a
syllable,
part of a word.
Fish – one syllable.
Face has one syllable.
Put them together and – hey!
It has two syllables – right, fishface?

David Orme

Tasks

 Write out the poems above and work out their syllable patterns. (The first has been started for you.)

Now, write out the following lantern poem, completing it with the correct number of syllables.

Rain

_____

Dripping down

_____

_____

2 Make up your own syllable pattern for a partner and ask them to write a poem, choosing from these subjects:

- the planet Mars
- an empty house
- making a cake
- a battery hen.

 3 On your own, work out the syllable patterns for the poems below. Write the pattern down. They are called **cinquains**. Why do you think this is?

Starlight
Waters dappling
Moonlight softly sleeping
Willows slowly sadly lapping
Weeping.

Phantom
Rattling your chains
And shrieking round my room
I will not be afraid of you
Depart!

 4 **Haiku**, a Japanese form of poetry, tries to capture a particular moment or experience. It generally has seventeen syllables set out in three lines. Read the following haiku:

As lightning flashes

Moonlight nightingale
Casts a whistling line of sand
Across the millpond.

Matsuo Basho

Kimono

A red kimono
Folded in a silk caress
Blushes with poppies.

Mary Green

Check if the haikus fit the pattern. Now write your own haiku using the picture above for ideas. (Strict haikus do not rhyme, but yours can, if you like.)

 5 Write a pyramid poem, a haiku and a cinquain on the same theme. Choose from these ideas or use your own:

- road-rage
- leaving home
- a pleasant surprise
- the view from the top of a mountain.

Further work

 6 Make up your own **alphabet** poem. It should have twenty-six lines (the number of letters in the alphabet) and a repeating pattern of syllables. For example, the following has one line of eleven syllables and one line of ten:

A is for alphabet, acrobat, apple,
B is for bungle, bovver and battle ...

Rhyme

> *The most common rhyme occurs when the sounds of word-endings match. It is found in poetry, song, jingles, rhyming slang and nursery rhymes. We sometimes rhyme by accident during conversations or find that we remember phrases or sayings because they rhyme.*

Read the following dialogue:

"A spot of bovver, las' night, I 'eard," said Billy. "Kenny lost 'is rag. Gave Freddie a slap."

"Nah!" replied George, laughing. "It was Freddie gave Kenny a slap ... in the mince-pie. And he knocked 'is barnet off."

"Well, well, would you Adam 'an Eve it! Jus' been on the dog 'an bone to Kenny's missus. She never said a dicky-bird about that."

"Serves Kenny right, if you ask me," George continued slowly and in hushed tones. "Nasty piece of work. 'E was the one what dumped Alfie in the Mona Lisa."

Tasks

 Discuss with a partner what the characters are like and what they are talking about in the dialogue above.

 When a word is replaced by other words that rhyme with it such as '**face/boat-race**' we call it rhyming slang.

List these words:

bother	**eye**	**believe**
telephone	**word**	**freezer**

Note down the words that match them from the passage above.
Write down what you think '**rag**' and '**barnet**' mean.
In pairs, discuss:

– how close you were to understanding the dialogue
– why you think people use rhyming slang.

 There are different kinds of rhymes. The easiest to recognise is the full rhyme or exact rhyme, such as **can/ran** or **late/rate**. It is the sound that matters, not the spelling. So, the words **Maisie/lazy** rhyme, although they are spelled differently. Copy out the table on the next page and fill the spaces with suitable words.

Word	Exact rhyme spelled the same	Exact rhyme spelled differently
shower		
coarse		
shore		
caught		
unfair		
report		
immense		
muscle		

 4 Some verses have lots of rhymes. Others have only a few. A poem with no rhymes at all is called blank verse.

Read the following and decide what kind of verses these are and where the rhymes occur (if at all). Think carefully when you are reading *In Watchful Community*.

I never saw a Purple Cow,
I never hope to see one;
But I can tell you, anyhow,
I'd rather see than be one.

Anon

In a small group, discuss the following:

– which is the more 'serious' poem?
– what is it describing?
– how does the rhyme suit the subject
  in each poem?

In Watchful Community
In watchful community
when we ought to be at school
sheltering by the warehouse
we stand, smelling
creosote, and the musty
rot of wood from floorboards
where sacks have lain, for
years, huddled together.

That is behind us, but
in front we hear the
plop of rain, and
while we stand
our bodies are increasing
in secret society.

Thom Gunn

Further work

 5 Make up rhyming slang for household objects such as a **table**, **chair**, **fridge**, **kettle** and so on. Use it to write a scene from a play about a family having breakfast. Include a character who doesn't understand what the family are talking about.

 6 What is the difference between **rhythm** and **rhyme**?
To help you answer, write out these lines. Underline the rhyme in red.

Here lies a man who was killed by lightning;
He died when his prospects seemed to be brightening.

Tap out the beat of each line – how many are there?

Other rhymes

> *Rhymes are used in different ways to create a range of moods. Nursery rhymes, chants and nonsense poetry have rhymes that are often repeated. This, along with a heavily stressed rhythm, helps to create humour and speed and makes the verse easy to remember.*

The House that Jack Built is a favourite rhyme with young children because the story is repeated as it is told. This is called **reiteration**.

Read this verse from it:

The House that Jack Built

This is the priest all shaven and shorn,
That married the man all tattered and torn,
That kissed the maiden all forlorn,
That milked the cow with the crumpled horn,
That tossed the dog,
That worried the cat,
That killed the rat,
That ate the malt,
That lay in the house that Jack built.

Full rhymes are one-syllable words in which the vowel and consonant rhyme.
Double rhymes have two rhymes.
Half rhymes have the same consonant rhyme at the end (kind/mend).
Internal rhymes are those which occur in the middle of a line.
End rhymes occur at the end of a line.

Tasks

 Discuss the verse above with a partner, making sure you understand the examples of rhymes and their definitions. Write down as many full, end, half, double and internal rhymes as you can. Are there any other rhymes which don't quite fit a definition but sound 'right'?

Make notes on the following:

– what else (apart from the rhyme) is repeated in the verse?
– what examples of alliteration are there (words beginning with the same sound)?
– what happens to the lines in the second half of the verse?
– how do these three points, along with the rhyme, have an effect on the way the story is told?

 Read this verse from *The Lady of Shalott* by Alfred Lord Tennyson.

There are many differences between it and *The House that Jack Built*, but there are also similarities.

In pairs, discuss:

– what word (rhyme) comes to mind when you read '**cried**'?
– what word meaning 'awful fate' rhymes with '**loom**', '**room**' and '**bloom**'?
– how do all these words and sounds fit the mood of the poem?

> She left the web, she left the loom,
> She made three paces thro' the room,
> She saw the water-lily bloom,
> She saw the helmet and the plume,
>   She look'd down to Camelot.
> Out flew the web and floated wide;
> The mirror crack'd from side to side;
> 'The curse is come upon me,' cried
>   The Lady of Shalott.

 Read these further definitions of rhymes:

– **triple rhyme** has three rhymes (for example **carnivorous/omnivorous**)
– **reverse rhyme** is like alliteration but more letters are the same (for example **shrimp/shrill**)
– **slant** or **off rhyme** has a different vowel sound (for example **ping-pong**).

Using these definitions, pair the following words and write down their names:

forget	**bicycle**	**pollination**	**photography**
stream	**examination**	**fell**	**dove**
streak	**tricycle**	**muddle**	**dive**
forward	**fall**	**topography**	**middle**

Further work

 The House that Jack Built is also an **accumulative** rhyme as it adds more detail as it builds up. Think of a subject and the things associated with it or a series of events beginning "On the first day ..." and write your own accumulative rhyme.

 Read the whole poem, *The Lady of Shalott*. Report to your teacher on the story it tells and the rhyme scheme.

Ellipsis

> *When we are talking to someone we often leave out words. It isn't necessary to keep repeating ourselves when the person we are talking to understands us. This omission of words is called ellipsis. Writers also use ellipsis to make dialogue sound convincing.*

Read the following:

(Errol enters looking flustered.)

Sue: Meena's just left.

Errol: For Brighton?

Sue: Yeah.

Errol: Did she say definitely?

Sue: Not exactly – but she mentioned Victoria Station.

Errol: Did she?

Sue: Yeah – and the one o'clock train.

Errol: Oh, well, she must have. How was she?

Sue: She said she'd ring later.

Errol: Did she? What – here?

Sue: Yeah. That's what she said.

Tasks

 Work with a partner. Decide what Sue and Errol are talking about (at least on the surface) and write out the dialogue putting in the information that has been left out.

    Sue: Meena's just left for Brighton.
    Errol: Meena's just left for Brighton?
    Sue: ...

When you have finished read it aloud. What does it sound like?

 Of course, we can leave out words in conversation because we don't want the person to know certain things.

Read the dialogue above again and discuss the situations with your partner.
Why is Errol flustered? Why has Meena gone?

Then write your own follow-up dialogue in which Meena rings either Sue or Errol.
Use ellipsis.

3 **Ellipsis dots** (...) are used by writers to show that part of a quotation has been left out.

For example:

The Prime Minister, who was in Scotland at the time, said the report was nonsense ...

becomes ...

The Prime Minister ... said the report was nonsense.

Read the following:

It is well known that hens, as well as other farm animals, need sufficient space to remain healthy and happy.

Write it out with a phrase missing. Put in ellipsis dots. Make sure the quotation still contains the main point.

Write your own sentence for a partner and ask them to rewrite it using ellipsis dots.

4 Sometimes words are left out or abbreviated in poetry and plays. This is called **elision** and is used to maintain the rhythm of a line.

Write out the quotations below and underline the word that has been changed. Then try to guess what the real word is and write it at the side.

Nature's first green is gold
Her hardest hue to hold,
Her early leaf's a flower ...

Robert Frost

And on that cheek and o'er the brow
So soft, so calm, yet eloquent,

Lord Byron

For I ne'er saw true beauty
    till this night.
Act I Scene V

'Tis but thy name that is my enemy.
Act II Scene II

Romeo and Juliet

William Shakespeare

Further work and revision

5 Write a scene from a story involving a bully being questioned by his/her parents. Include a dialogue that has ellipsis and hidden meanings.

6 Re-read Byron's two lines. How many syllables are there in each? How many 'stresses' are there in each?

Spelling

English is a rich language as a result of the different influences on it, but it has also presented us with a complex spelling system. Most of us have problems remembering certain words. Many are not spelled as they sound, some look the same but are spelled differently, while others sound the same but have different spellings and meanings (homophones).

Read the following verse:

English Spelling Blues

I never remember if it's where or wear,
There, their or they're or hair, hare or heir,
I strugle for hours over through and threw,
And forget the speling of knew and new.
My wrighting's a mess, my brother says so,
I'm bound to confuse even know and no – he says.
Bald and bawled is well beyond me,
And fysics and sykicks just eztrawdinry.
I knead to think strate, I'll begin agen,
I wearily, warily pick up my pen.
But my head's in a mudle, I hate this stuff,
So I'm chuckin' this work 'cos I've had enuff – I say.

(P.S. I think it's time to forget this rime, two.)

Mary Green

Tasks

1. Write down all the homophones in the verse. Choose three and make up rhymes or jokes to show their different meanings.

   For example:
   I'm brushing my hare!

2. Discuss with a partner what method the writer has used to spell the word, 'extraordinary'. What is wrong with using this method here? Can you think of a better one?

   On your own, find other spelling mistakes in the verse, write them out correctly and check them in a dictionary.

3 The following words are often used in different school subjects. Match the words to their meanings and say which subject they belong to. (A word may belong to more than one subject.)

Key words	Meanings
1. tempo	A. distance around something
2. sources	B. the larger community
3. parallel	C. speed and rhythm
4. narrative	D. information to indicate proof
5. evidence	E. story
6. society	F. running side by side but not meeting
7. circumference	G. turn into moisture
8. evaporate	H. origins or beginnings

Write down your answers like this: **1.C.** (Music)

Now work with a partner to see if you can spell the key words correctly. Split the words into their syllables first. You will find it easier to remember them. Then test each other.

 4 Plurals – adding 's' to words that end in 'y'.

Read the plurals below. Write down the singular for each one and work out the spelling rule:

keys	**cherries**	**parties**	**donkeys**
trolleys	**countries**	**journeys**	**rubies**
daisies	**toys**	**turkeys**	**counties**
valleys	**lorries**	**diaries**	**cowboys**

To make the plural of these words you add 's':

cuff   cliff   chief   giraffe   roof   proof   belief   reef

To make the plural of these words you drop the 'f' or 'fe' and add 'ves'.

calf   half   life   wife   knife   leaf   loaf   wolf   shelf

Write down the plurals of the words in both lists.

They are difficult to remember, so try to use them in your writing and keep a record of them in a spelling diary.

Further work

 5 Look at the headlines below which are based on two plurals from the list above. Write the news reports to go with them; make sure you use the plurals correctly.

– Cherry's cherries keep growing!
– Parties send Daisy off her trolley!

Find out what is unusual about the plurals of these words:
hoof   scarf   wharf

Mnemonics

> Mnemonics (pronounced 'nemonics') are devices to help you remember things, such as difficult spellings. For example, a mnemonic for the word 'length' could be:
>
> <u>l</u>azy <u>e</u>lephants <u>n</u>ever <u>g</u>o <u>t</u>o <u>h</u>eaven

You could, of course, make up a mnemonic just for the part that you get wrong, like this:

Mistake	Correct spelling	Mnemonic
len<u>gh</u>t	len<u>gth</u>	great <u>t</u>in <u>h</u>ats
n<u>es</u>sary	ne<u>cess</u>ary	<u>c</u>losed <u>e</u>yes <u>s</u>ee <u>s</u>pots

Tasks

 Read these mnemonics and write down what spellings they stand for:

- all new sweethearts wear emerald rings

- gorillas often enjoy scratching

- a little wish and you smile

- baby insects softly cuddle up in turnips.

 Write down your own mnemonics for these words.
(They are words we often misspell.)

       ghost   **also**   **fulfil**   **diary**

Putting difficult spellings in a passage is another way of learning them. Read this example:

They had already started their meal when Mum arrived back. "Is it absolutely necessary to watch television when you're eating?" she asked.
"Of course, Mum," replied Andy. "All our friends do – and they're allowed; Joe's mum thought you ought to let us, too."
"It's none of her business!" cried Mum, "... and, while we're on the subject, who's eaten all the biscuits?"
"Crumbs!" said Andy to his brother, "... let's scarper!"

List the words from the passage that are likely to be misspelled. Look carefully – not all are long words.
Get a friend to read the passage to you slowly. See if you can write it out correctly.

 List words you commonly misspell – or ones from this page – and put them in a short passage from a story (check they're spelled correctly). Then get a friend to dictate it to you.

 Work with a partner. Give each other spelling tests on the geographical words below:

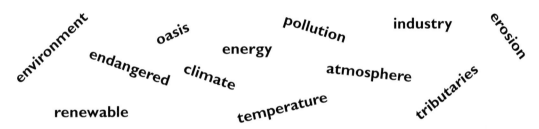

Mark each other's work and make up mnemonics for the parts of the words you got wrong.

 Here are two other ways of remembering spellings:

To spell '**friend**' you could say:
'**Fri**day comes at the **end** of the week.'

To spell '**Egypt**' you could say each letter aloud and add a rhyme like this:
E   G   Y   P   T
The place I'd like to be.

Choose three words you often misspell and make up sayings for them.

Further work

 LCWC is a way of learning spellings. What do you think it stands for?

Tests

> *The following exercises will test you on what you have learned in Section 2.*

 1 Write down each sound pattern with the correct example.

Sound pattern	**Example**
1. Alliteration	A. POW!
2. Onomatopoeia	B. reference/preference
3. Full rhyme	C. went/mint
4. Half rhyme	D. mad/lad
5. Double rhyme	E. singing softly
6. Triple rhyme	F. Ronald/Donald

 2 Copy out the following passage, which uses alliteration and onomatopoeia, supplying your own words to fit the spaces:

The enraged seagull swiftly s-(...) **down onto the unsuspecting passer-by, Arthur Morton, who raised his umbrella to defend himself. The seagull** s-(...) **loudly, causing the parrots in the nearby pet-shop to** s-(...) **with such a din that the owner rushed outside.**
"O-(...)!" cried the wounded pedestrian, as the seagull pecked him on the nose. "It's defending its chicks," explained the pet-shop owner, "your umbrella must have frightened it!"
The next day's local paper headline read: 'A s- (...) seagull a- (...) A-(...).'

 3 Copy and complete this poem of one and two syllable lines repeated.

The	(one syllable)
_ _ _ _ _ _	(two syllables)
_ _ _	
street lamp	
_ _ _	
_ _ _ _ _ _	

4 This is a syllable poem crossword.
The answers to the crossword are jumbled-up.
Correct them.

Across
1. Five line poem that says its name.

Down
2. This poem gives light.
3. Seventeen syllable poem from Japan.

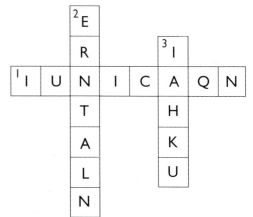

© Folens

Write out these sentences, choosing the correct spelling.

- He lost his grip on the **peddle/pedal** and the bike hurtled to the **right/write**.

- I like wild and windy **weather/whether** and days of **piece/peace** and solitude.

- They weren't **sure/shore** if the costumes for the second **seen/scene** had arrived.

- He **new/knew** he had to mix the **yolk/yoke** with the **flour/flower** and butter.

- She held the **rain/rein/reign** tightly as the **hoarse/horse** galloped forward.

- Errol bought three boxes of **serial/cereal**, some **leeks/leaks** and a **pare/pair/pear**.

 Write mnemonics for these words:

yolk   **rein**   **flour**   **pear**

Ellipsis

 Read the following:

- Her presence, despite the family's irritation, was like a breath of fresh air.

- He played every shot, despite his bad ankle, as if his life depended on it.

- Winston, although he had an IQ of 120, regularly came last in Scrabble and Monopoly.

Rewrite these sentences using ellipsis dots to show the words that can be left out. Make sure the sentences still contain the main points.

 Rewrite the following dialogue in full sentences where ellipsis occurs:

Jo: Been out?
Steve: Might have.
Jo: What you up to?
Steve: Not a lot.
Jo: You liar. Know what I think?
Steve: What?
Jo: You've been looking for a secret Valentine's present for me.
Steve: Supposed to be a surprise.
Jo: Can't keep anything from me, Steve. Known each other too long.
Steve: Then how come you didn't spot the new puppy?
Jo: New puppy? You're joking!
Steve: Here, boy! (*opens door, puppy bounds in*).

Longer assignments

Below are a number of longer assignments based on what you have learned in Section 2. Part One contains two compulsory tasks, Part Two gives you a choice of several assignments.

Part One: Compulsory

 Read the poems below. Note the different sound patterns that occur in each poem. Think about different types of rhyme, line length, alliteration, onomatopoeia and so on.

a)
Suicide in the Trenches

I knew a simple soldier boy
Who grinned at life in empty joy,
Slept soundly through the lonesome dark,
And whistled early with the lark.

In winter trenches, cowed and glum,
With crumps and lice and lack of rum,
He put a bullet through his brain.
No one spoke of him again.

You smug-faced crowds with kindling eye
Who cheer when soldier lads march by,
Sneak home and pray you'll never know
The hell where youth and laughter go.

Siegfried Sassoon (a soldier in the First World War)

b)
Sea Timeless Song

Hurricane come
and hurricane go
but sea ... sea timeless
sea timeless
sea timeless
sea timeless
sea timeless

Hibiscus bloom
then dry-wither so
but sea ... sea timeless
sea timeless
sea timeless
sea timeless
sea timeless

Tourist come
and tourist go
but sea ... sea timeless
sea timeless
sea timeless
sea timeless
sea timeless

Grace Nichols

c)
Lucy Locket lost her pocket,
Kitty Fisher found it;
There was not a penny in it.
Only ribbon round it.

Nursery rhyme 1700s

 Write about each of the poems. Say:

- what the sound pattern is
- how the sound patterns add to the meaning of the poems.

Part Two

Choose one of the following:

 Make your own poetry anthology.

Write at least three poems of your own. Each should use a range of sound patterns and forms. Remember syllable and shape poems as well as different types of rhyme and sound. Experiment with different line lengths.

Include at least two poems written by other poets which show a range of sound patterns. You may need to do some library research for this.

Write a short introduction describing the poems you've written and chosen and what sound patterns are used in them (and why).

 Devise a spelling-tips book. It should contain pages on the following:

- mnemonics
- methods for remembering words such as the <u>L</u>ook, <u>C</u>over, <u>W</u>rite, <u>C</u>heck method
- spelling rules
- special subject words (for Geography, Science and so on).

Here are some examples for remembering spellings:

> - If you keep spelling a word wrongly, highlight the hard part:
> **precipetation X**   **precipi<u>it</u>ation**

> - Write down simpler words or the letter string alongside:
> **precip<u>it</u>ation   it   pit**

> - Split long words into parts:
> **at   mos   phere**

Leave blank pages so you can add more tips.

Longer assignments: Section 2

Setting personal targets

 Look through the work you did in Section 2 and make a list of the things you did not understand or did not do very well. Keep your list to refer to.

 Talk to your teacher, and choose at least three and no more than five of the following targets to meet. Make sure you choose both reading and writing targets. Use your list to help you choose.

Alliteration

- When I am reading poems I will try to recognise alliteration.
- When I am writing about poems I will use the term and say how it adds to the meaning of the poem.
- When I am writing my own poems I will use alliteration.

Onomatopoeia

- I will try to recognise how onomatopoeia is used in poems, comics and advertisements.
- When I am writing about sound patterns I will use the term and say how it adds to the meaning of poems, jingles and other work.
- When I am writing my own poems I will try to use onomatopoeia when appropriate.

Syllable patterns

- When I am reading poems I will try to recognise different syllable patterns.
- When I am writing about poems I will use the different names for syllable poems and say how syllable patterns add to the meaning.
- When I am writing I will use a variety of syllable poems and also make up my own syllable patterns for poems.

Rhymes

- When I am reading poems I will try to recognise the different rhymes.
- When I am writing about poems I will use the correct terms and say how the rhyme scheme adds to the meaning of the poem.
- When I am writing my own poems I will use a variety of rhymes, not just obvious ones.

Ellipsis

● When I am reading I will try to recognise ellipsis in dialogues.
● When I am writing about dialogues I will try to say how ellipsis makes the dialogue sound convincing.
● When I am writing my own dialogues I will try to use ellipsis convincingly.
● When I am referring to a quotation from a book I will use ellipsis dots, where appropriate, to show that words have been left out.

Elision

● When I am reading poems and plays, particularly those by Shakespeare and other pre-twentieth-century writers, I will try to recognise how elision adds to the rhythm.
● When I see elision being used I will try to work out what the full meaning of the word is (for example, o'er = over).

Spelling

● I will check that I understand what homophones are and try to spell them correctly, particularly common ones such as 'there', 'their', and 'they're'.
● I will try to remember useful spelling rules, particularly those to do with plurals.
● I will record some spellings every day, particularly words I'm not sure of and also key words.

Mnemonics

● I will make up mnemonics for common spellings I often get wrong.

Simple and complex sentences

When we want to say something in writing we use sentences. Sentences can be simple or complex. A simple sentence (or clause) might be a statement such as: 'I love food' or 'He can run very fast'. As sentences become more complex, saying what we mean becomes more difficult.

Read the following:

Dear Molly,

We're arrived at the cottage! Rover is fine and Dan too but I have to keep him in the shed until I get things straight and check him for fleas before I let him in. He's not very pleased. You know how he likes to fetch his paper and curl up on my lap as if he was an old dog! Never mind, he got a bone today and a good run with the old stick so he can't complain.

The weather is sunny. The beach is sandy.

Wish you were here

Millie

P.S. Remember, when the parrot won't eat his chewy, chop it into little pieces and put it in the bowl belonging to Maisie with the chipped handle.

MOLLY JONES
92 HIGH STREET
HAPPYTOWN
SMILESHIRE

HN2 2AB.

Tasks

 Read the postcard again and copy down three simple sentences.

Now list all the points Millie makes that are unclear.

Check your list with two other people and add any more points you may have left out.

Rewrite Millie's postcard so that it makes sense.

You can change the order of the words, but try to include all the points Millie is making.

 A **simple** sentence is **one main clause**. The main clause generally has a **subject**, a **verb** and usually an **object**. Look at the sentence '**I love food**' again:

Subject	Verb	Object
(a noun or pronoun) I	(action word) love	(a noun or pronoun) food

Copy out the table above and add the subjects, verbs and objects from these three sentences.

– The wind blew the trees.
– He rang the bell.
– Fireflies hovered in the air.

 Complex sentences usually have a **subordinate clause** and may contain **phrases** which provide further information.
The subordinate clause gives more important information than the phrase in the sentence – although this is not always easy to work out!

Subordinate clause	Main clause	Phrase
When she arrives,	I will bake a cake	with these fresh eggs.

Copy out the sentence below:

He is absent because he has gone away with his family.

With a partner, separate the sentence using a table like the one above.

Now copy these down and work them out on your own.

– They left on their horses as the sun rose.
– She agreed that he was right about the incident.

Write three sentences of your own. Include a subordinate clause and a phrase in each one. Make sure the meaning of each sentence is clear.

Further work

 Write two versions of the same postcard. It should be written by Molly in reply to Millie's postcard. (See opposite page.)
The first version should be clear and well written, the second should be unclear and funny.
Use **simple** and **complex** sentences when you write.

Other labels

Connectives

> *Connectives (or linking words and phrases) are used to join clauses. They help us to present more complex ideas and to give more information. Common connectives are: 'and', 'but', 'or', 'so', 'for', 'when', 'from', 'in'. There are many others.*

Look at the following and read the sentences below:

Biff, a one-year-old mongrel, was rescued from drowning at Bognor beach in Sussex on Monday by his owner, Sam Dare, a fit fifty-year-old.
"I couldn't let my wife down. She loves Biff," said Sam.

Tasks

 Write down all the connectives in the first sentence and say what kind of information they help to give us about the incident. For example, we are told where the incident happened.

 Imagine you are a photographer. You are at a special event such as the start of a balloon race or a World Cup match. Draw three pictures. Write one sentence describing what's happening using four or more connectives. Make sure your sentence is clear and easy to read.

Connectives can be a group of words as well as single words.
For example:

'as far as'   'similar to'   'such as'   'except that'
                                                    'rather than'

'as though'   'so that'   'in order that'   'different from'

Take each one of the above in turn and write a sentence using the phrase, adding another connective that you know, such as:

He finished his tea quickly **so that** he could meet his friends **before** the park shut.

 Connect each list of ideas below to make one sentence. You may need to drop some words and change the order. You should have three sentences in all.

Tariq loved ice-skating.
His friends preferred roller-skating.
They went with Tariq every week.

The football was on Saturday.
She was going to the match.
Her friends were keen supporters.

Darren's grandmother made his tea every Friday.
Darren was going to the pictures.
Darren would buy some fish and chips.

Further work and revision

 Choose one set of ideas from Task 1 or Task 4 and write a full account of what happened. Include other events, when they happened and why.

 Remember **homophones?**
Read these two sentences. Decide what is wrong with them and write them out correctly. There are five mistakes. Underline any connectives.

– The see was calm, the peer silent and the beech deserted, so I had a swim.
– The waive rose higher and higher, then crashed on to the sure.

The naming of parts

You will already be familiar with nouns, verbs and other parts of speech. The term, 'parts of speech' is one of the most common ways of describing types of words and what they do.

Read the following poem:

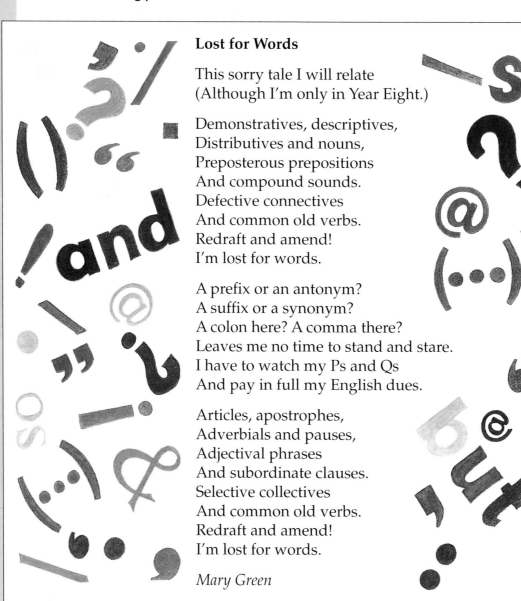

Lost for Words

This sorry tale I will relate
(Although I'm only in Year Eight.)

Demonstratives, descriptives,
Distributives and nouns,
Preposterous prepositions
And compound sounds.
Defective connectives
And common old verbs.
Redraft and amend!
I'm lost for words.

A prefix or an antonym?
A suffix or a synonym?
A colon here? A comma there?
Leaves me no time to stand and stare.
I have to watch my Ps and Qs
And pay in full my English dues.

Articles, apostrophes,
Adverbials and pauses,
Adjectival phrases
And subordinate clauses.
Selective collectives
And common old verbs.
Redraft and amend!
I'm lost for words.

Mary Green

Tasks

 Work with a partner. List all the parts of speech and punctuation you recognise in the poem above and make a note of what they mean alongside.

Write sentences that use the parts of speech in your list. You must:

– connect your sentences around one idea (such as: 'eating ice-cream on a hot day')
– cover at least five parts of speech.

 When we want to compare two or more objects we sometimes add '**more**' and '**most**' to adjectives:

Adjective	Comparative (used with two objects)	Superlative (used with more than two objects)
comfortable	This seat is <u>more comfortable</u> than that one.	This seat is the <u>most comfortable</u> of all.

Sometimes the original word changes:

great ⟶ greater ⟶ greatest

Draw a table like this. Make comparatives and superlatives for each word and write them in the boxes. Think carefully about whether or not the word changes.

Adjective	Comparative	Superlative
small		
thin		
famous		
careful		
beautiful		

 Adverbs work in a similar way:

– early, earlier, earliest
– carefully, more carefully, most carefully.

Write a set of comparative and superlative sentences using the words below.

happily   greedily   easily   soon

Further work

 Write a poem about the difficulties of writing well. Think of spelling and handwriting as well as parts of speech and punctuation. Try to include a comment on the problems of finding the 'right' word and use some of the comparatives and superlatives you have made on this page.

Other labels

Using the dash

The dash can be used in more than one way – but it has to be used carefully. You will see from the sentence written above that the dash can be used like a comma. It separates two parts of a sentence rather like a comma and provides a pause or interruption. It can also add emphasis or drama.

Read the following:

The telephone rings. Sue picks it up.
There is interference on the line.

Sue:	Hello.
Caller:	Can I speak to Cheryl, please?
Sue:	Sorry – what did you say?
Caller:	Can I speak to Cheryl, please?
Sue:	Who?
Caller:	Cheryl – I want to speak to Cheryl.
Sue:	Gerald? There's no Gerald here.
Caller:	Not Gerald – Cheryl – CHERYL!
Sue:	Oh! Errol! Sorry – Errol doesn't live here.

Caller gives up in desperation.

Meena,
Your Mum says can you collect the clothes from the cleaners – red coat, black jacket – and don't forget to feed the cat.
See you later, Errol.

Tasks

1 With a partner, discuss the different ways in which the dash is being used in the examples above. Then write four sentences of your own using the dash and ask your partner to check them.

2 Using the dash, write two messages. One from Sue to Errol explaining that she thinks an ex-girlfriend has been trying to contact him and the other from Meena to Errol in reply to his note.

Read the following from *The Posthumous Papers of the Pickwick Club* by Charles Dickens. Mr Pickwick and his friends are leaving an inn by coach.

"Heads, heads – take care of your heads," cried the loquacious stranger, as they came out under the low archway, which in those days formed the entrance to the coachyard. "Terrible place–dangerous work–other day– five children–mother–tall lady, eating sandwiches–forgot the arch–crash– knock–children look round–mother's head off–sandwich in her hand–no mouth to put it in–head of a family off–shocking, shocking!"

Write down the answers to the following questions and then compare them with a partner's.

What does the use of the dash tell you about the character speaking?
Do you think your teacher would like it if you always wrote like this?
How does the dash add to the humour?

 Write a comic paragraph using dashes. Include an interesting character and choose one of these situations:

the final minutes of a match when your team has lost

losing a shoe in the street

finding out a friendly dog has fleas

being caught in a violent thunderstorm

dropping pocket-money down the drain

offering excuses about being late to your teacher

Further work and revision

Write a story about a day when everything goes wrong. Develop some of the work you have done already on these pages.

Colons and semicolons

> *The colon is a pause which is most often used to list information or give examples and explanations. For example:*
>
> *To do the job properly you will need: a spanner, a drill, a hammer and a screwdriver.*

You will see in the example above that the colon has been used to introduce a list.

The colon can also be used in dialogue to indicate that a character is speaking. In pairs, read the following as a script:

The bank manager's office.
A customer enters.

Bank Manager: Well, well. Take a seat, take a seat.

Customer: Thank you. It's about the loan, Mr ... er?

Bank Manager: Piddleton, Piddleton's the name *(looking at some papers and muttering to himself)*. This won't do, won't do at all, Mr Slacker.

Customer: But ...

Bank Manager: I have a list here, Mr Slacker, a list as long as your arm; a list, I might say, of misdemeanours. I have: the bounced cheque from Piddleton's DIY – yes, Piddleton's, Mr Slacker – the bicycle clamp project which never got on the road, the failed PAY-AND-GO venture and *(shuffling more papers)* – yes – here we are – the Grimaldi ice-cream debt.

Customer: But hang on ...

Bank Manager: And that, Mr Slacker, is just for starters! Look at this. *(Holds up another paper.)* It says: no payment to account, February, March, April, despite numerous reminders; £500 deposited last Monday, withdrawn Tuesday. I ask you, Mr Slacker, I ask you!

Customer: But hang on, Mr Piddleton ...

Bank Manager: Hang on? Hang on? You're here, Mr Slacker, requesting a loan, a loan. Well, no can do, Mr Slacker, no can do!

Customer: I'm ... I'm outraged. I shall be removing my account, forthwith.

Bank Manager: Removing your account? At this rate, Mr Slacker, I think we'll be removing it for you. What d'you say to that, eh?

Customer: Say? Say? I have one thing to say to you, Mr Piddleton and one thing only. My name's not Slacker!

Tasks

1   Read the dialogue again and write down the different ways the colon is used. Then, write a sentence that includes a list, such as a list of what you'd like for your birthday, a list of jobs or homework that needs doing. Use the colon.

2   Work with a partner. Look at the situations below or think of your own. Write a dialogue, taking the part of one character each. Try to make your dialogue funny. Use the colon in more than one way.

   – A customer complaining to a travel company about a holiday.
   – A newsagent giving instructions to a newspaper boy about his round.
   – The bride's father working out the wedding menu with the caterer.

Semicolons

When we are writing we may want to show that two ideas, facts or events are closely linked. We can use a semicolon to do this. For example:

The kitchen was as bright as a new pin; his grandfather was a stickler for cleanliness.

Pair the following sentences:

   – He was already an hour late.   – It was a well-earned rest.
   – She's not an aggressive person.   – She only loses her temper sometimes.
   – It was time to take it easy.   – She was bound to be worried.

Now rewrite them to make three sentences separated by a semicolon. (You do not need a capital after a semicolon.)

4   In a more complicated sentence, especially if we are listing information, we can use the semicolon to separate the main parts of the sentence:

She emptied both pockets: in the right was a toothbrush, a comb, a piece of chocolate and a toffee; in the left, a chewed pencil, her pet spider and – at last – the missing key!

Find examples of the semicolon in the 'bank-manager' script. Write down why they have been used and then write two sentences of your own to show both uses of the semicolon. Look at the example above again. Write down any other punctuation that has been used, explaining why it has been chosen.

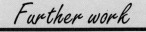

Further work

5   One Friday morning, Meena, Sue and Errol witness a bank robbery in the local high street, but they all have slightly different accounts of what happened. Write the three accounts. Include the date, time and location of the robbery and use colons, semicolons and commas to help you present each account clearly. Begin by drawing a brief sketch map of the high street, location of the bank, side streets and anything else that you think is important.

More naming of parts

Two of the most common parts of speech are the definite article (the) and the indefinite article (a/an). These words are probably among the first you learned to write. Other names for some commonly-used words are demonstratives (this, that, these).

Read the following proverbs. They are sometimes called wise sayings and give advice about life in general.

A. Where there's a will there's a way.
B. Don't throw the baby out with the bath water.
C. The least said the soonest mended.
D. One swallow doesn't make a summer.
E. A cat may look at a king.
F. Absence makes the heart grow fonder.
G. We never miss the water until the well runs dry.
H. A friend in need is a friend indeed.
I. A hungry man is an angry man.

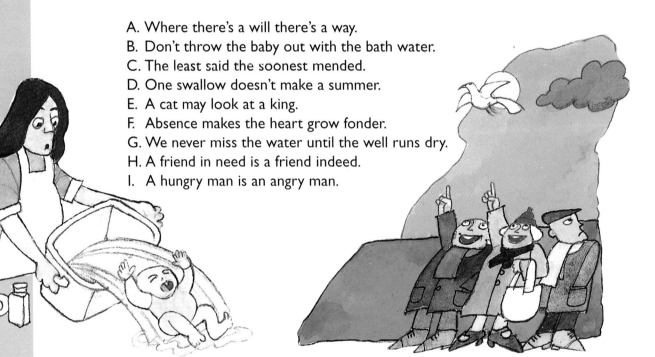

Tasks

 Discuss with a partner what the proverbs mean and whether or not you agree with them.

 Find all the definite and indefinite articles.
Read each proverb without them. Which still make sense?
Now swap over 'the' with 'a' or 'an' and vice versa in each proverb.
Make notes on the differences these changes make.
Decide whether the proverbs have been improved.

 If we were to use 'the' and 'a' all the time our writing would become very boring.
Demonstratives enable us to give more information. They are useful when we want to refer to the nearness or distance of something.

This book ... (the book nearby)
That book ... (the book further away)

Read the proverbs again. Replace 'the' and 'a' with 'this' or 'that'. Decide what has happened to the proverbs by copying down the table below and ticking the boxes. Tick more than one box if you wish and add your comments in the last column about how the meanings have changed.

Proverbs	Still makes sense	No longer makes sense	Sounds odd	Sounds better	Other information
A					
B					
C					
D					
E					
F					
G					
H					
I					

Make up four of your own proverbs using the definite and indefinite article and the demonstrative.

 Hyphens

You have already met the dash. Another name for a dash is a **hyphen**, but it has a different function. Hyphens are used to join words together, for example: **brown-eyed**, **short-haired**.

Put the hyphen in the correct places in these sentences:

– In the museum he saw a three hundred year old shoe and a T shirt dated 1950.

– He could not decide between the ruby red velvet or the sky blue silk.

– Luckily, she only bruised her shoulder blade when she crashed her motorbike.

Rewrite these sentences without the hyphen. You will need to reorganise the words.

– She was an unknown nineteenth-century artist.

– A well-liked neighbour was moving to another town.

Further work

5 Take one of the proverbs from page 46 and use it as the title of a story, using a variety of demonstratives.

Apostrophes to shorten words

> The apostrophe is used when we shorten words. It replaces the letters that have been left out, like this:
>
> let's   let us (let'~~u~~s)
>
> We call this using the apostrophe for omission.

Read the following:

Thursday evening, 6.40pm. Errol is waiting for Meena outside the Odeon. Suddenly, Meena comes around the corner, running.

Errol: Where've you been?

Meena: Sorry!

Errol: You're forty minutes late. We agreed six o'clock!

Meena: I know, I'm sorry. It wasn't my fault.

Errol: I've been waiting ages.

Meena: Well, I forgot my money. Then ...

Errol: The queue's a mile long and he *(meaning the manager, Mr O'Brien)* wouldn't let me in unless I'd got tickets already. I'd really planned on seeing this film, y'know.

Meena: *(sighing)* It'll be alright. I expect we'll get in.
(The manager comes out and Meena turns to him.) Excuse me, can you tell us if there are still seats for ... *(turning to Errol)* What's it called?

Errol: *Dead on Time.*

Manager: *Dead on Time?* *(laughing)* Yes, you'll make it. Move along, please.

Meena: Then, you see, I borrowed Sue's bike 'cause I knew I'd be late and you wouldn't believe it, I'd just turned the corner when ... *(she breaks off)* ... you're not listening, Errol.

Errol: *(He is pointing)* Look! That's all I need!
(The manager is coming out again, carrying a large placard. He places it on the steps in front of Meena and Errol. It reads: SORRY FOLKS! DEAD ON TIME 7PM PERFORMANCE POSTPONED. NEXT PERFORMANCE 8.30PM.)

Tasks

 Work with a partner. List all the examples of the apostrophe (showing omission) that you can find and write the full version alongside. Some examples are repeated (for example, I had – I'd).

Find an example of the apostrophe used in another way, in the passage.

2 Correct the following. Five apostrophes have been put in the wrong places.

"Weve decided to run this film for another two weeks'," said Mr OBrien to the box office clerk.

"Its been very popular. Therell be queues' in the aisles' soon," replied Mr Sims'. "Though it isnt one of my favourites'," he added.

 3 Decide whether or not these should have an apostrophe and why:

fraid so	Kate ODonald	As and Bs	Halloween
the 1970s	freebie	bout five	ifs and buts

Check your answers with a partner.

 4 Read the incomplete telephone conversation below. Think about the possible missing lines.

First Friend: Are you going to the party tomorrow?

Second Friend:

F.F. Why not?

S.F.

F.F. Everyone else is going.

S.F.

F.F. What a pity.

S.F.

F.F. Try again.

S.F.

F.F. Go on, ask nicely.

S.F.

F.F. Well, good luck. Ring me tomorrow.

Now copy and complete the conversation by writing in sentences and using the apostrophe.

Further work and revision

 5 Write a dialogue between Mr O'Brien (the manager of the cinema) and the box office clerk about the film, *Dead On Time* and its postponement. Use the apostrophe.

 6 Write a short review about a film you have seen. Use comparatives and superlatives such as 'sadder' or 'funniest'.

Apostrophes for ownership

> The apostrophe is also used to show ownership – that something belongs to something else.
>
> The words belonging to the <u>singer</u> were changed.
> The singer's words were changed.
>
> If we were talking about more than one singer we would write:
>
> The words belonging to the <u>singers</u> were changed.
> The singers' words were changed.

Now read through this weather report:

Devon Deluge

Yesterdays thunderstorms brought havoc to Devons tourist resorts. Three inches of rain fell in an hour. The River Otters banks overflowed at several spots and flood warnings were issued. Thousands of holiday-makers cars ground to a halt as traffic jams multiplied and tourists tempers frayed.

Heavy rain is expected again tomorrow and farmers worries are justified since crops could be damaged.

One local residents view sums up this summer crisis: a washout!

© Folens

Tasks

 Work with a partner. The apostrophe (showing possession) is missing from seven words in the weather report. Write the mistakes, and the corrections next to them.

 Write your own report of a storm hitting a village. Use these phrases:

weathermen's chart **hurricane's path** **buildings' roofs**

 When the plural has no 's' and we want to use the apostrophe we treat it as though it was singular. For example:

women's **men's**

Proper names and groups can also use the singular:

The Wong family's party **Jack and Jill's pail**

Pair the phrases that use the apostrophe in the same way in this scattergram. Write them out correctly.

> the peoples palace   childrens books
>
> Sue and Meenas day-out   The River Tweeds estuary
>
> The Tate Gallerys exhibition   Simon and Errols bike

 Copy out lists A and B, then pair the words on each side. Experiment with interesting combinations, before you decide on your final choice.

A	B
Youth's	wisdom
Beauty's	song
Age's	eye
Fame's	optimism
Love's	brevity

With a partner, discuss which choices work best. Now add the words below to List A and match them with your own words added to List B.

Art's **Friendship's** **Nature's** **Death's** **Music's**

Further work

 You have recently returned from holiday. Write a letter to a friend explaining how your luggage, which contained presents for your family, got swapped for someone else's by mistake. Use the apostrophe for omission and possession.

Direct speech

> Direct speech is an account of the actual words spoken by someone and inverted commas (speech marks) are used to contain the words. Any words that are not spoken remain outside:
>
> "I need a holiday!" she sighed.

Read the following:

Meena raced along the street towards the house where Sue lived. She ran up the path and pressed the doorbell. There was no reply. She rang the bell several times in quick succession. Finally, she heard some footsteps and Sue opened the door.

"What on earth's the matter?" Sue asked.

"Oh! Thank goodness you're in! Can I borrow your bike? I'm in a real hurry," gasped Meena.

"Come in first and catch your breath," continued Sue. She ushered Meena into the hall. "Yeah, of course you can borrow it, but I warn you, it's a rusty old thing."

"I don't care. Anything's better than nothing. I'm fifteen minutes late as it is." Sue took Meena to the small garden at the back of the house and there, propped up against the wall, was a bike. It had definitely seen better days.

"It's not much to look at," said Sue, "but it works and the brakes are good." Meena grabbed the bike and wheeled it round to the front of the house.

"Thanks, you're a real pal!" she called out, as she pedalled off.

Tasks

 In the speech bubbles below are the first words spoken by Sue and Meena. Write out the rest of the conversation in the same way, using speech bubbles. Remember, only write down the actual words that are spoken in the speech bubbles.

Imagine Meena has doubts about the bike. Write a short conversation between her and Sue. If you need to, start by using speech bubbles, then use inverted commas as you progress.

 There are other important features in the layout of the speech.
Look at the punctuation below.

"_____," she said.   "_____?" she asked.

"_____!" she exclaimed.

Write down where the commas, full-stops, question marks and exclamation marks are in these examples.

Look at the passage on page 52. In pairs, answer the following questions:

– What happens to the spacing each time someone else speaks?
– What is the punctuation and spacing like when someone starts speaking, stops, then starts again in the same sentence?

Make notes about speech layout. Try to remember them when you use direct speech.

 Single inverted commas are used in books but in handwritten work we use double inverted commas. Single inverted commas are also used in other ways:

– For speech within speech:
   Errol said, "What did he mean when he said 'tomorrow at 4.30'?"

– Around titles, such as books and films:
   'Star Wars'   **'Romeo and Juliet'**

Write out the following using single and double inverted commas correctly.

Errol read out his short story to the rest of the class. He enjoyed science fiction and the story was rather like *Earth Is Room Enough* by Isaac Asimov. When he had finished the teacher said, Well done, Errol. I particularly like the part where you say the mechanical teacher had broken down!

Further work

 Either:
write a conversation between Meena and a passer-by whom Meena almost knocks over while she is riding Sue's bike. The bike is damaged and the passer-by is particularly cross because of its poor condition.

or:
write a conversation between two people such as a footballer and a referee or a head-teacher and a pupil.

Use direct speech and if you wish, start by writing the spoken words in speech bubbles.

Indirect speech

> *Indirect (or reported) speech is an account of what has been said. It does not contain inverted commas (speech marks), nor does it have to contain the actual words. It should, however, have the same meaning.*

The following is Sue and Meena's conversation on page 52 written in indirect speech.

Meena raced along the street towards the house where Sue lived. She ran up the path and pressed the doorbell. There was no reply. She rang the bell several times in quick succession. Finally, she heard some footsteps and Sue opened the door. Seeing Meena in a panic, she asked her what on earth the matter was. Meena, relieved to see that Sue was in, replied that she needed a bike as quickly as possible. After calming her down, Sue ushered Meena into the hall. She said that of course Meena could have the bike, but warned her that it was old and rusty. Meena said that she didn't care and that anything was better than nothing because she was already fifteen minutes late.

Sue took Meena to the small garden at the back of the house. There, propped up against the wall was the bike, which had definitely seen better days. She pointed out, that although the bike was not much to look at, it worked and the brakes were good.

Meena grabbed the bike, wheeled it around to the front of the house and, calling out her thanks to Sue, saying that she was a real pal, pedalled off.

Tasks

 Work with a partner. Compare the report above with Sue and Meena's conversation on page 52.

List the ways in which the direct speech has been changed to become indirect speech. Look for key phrases like this:

Direct speech	Indirect speech
"Oh! Thank goodness you're in ..."	Meena, relieved to see that Sue was in ...

 Rewrite these sentences using indirect speech. Underline the words you change or add.

Sue said, "If we go soon, we'll get to Blackpool before one o'clock."
"Let's take sandwiches and cake with us," replied Meena. "That way we won't need to buy any food," she added.

The following are in indirect speech. Rewrite them in direct speech.

– He asked his sister if he could borrow her computer.

– She told us yesterday that the dog had gone to a good home.

– He said that he would make the family a special curry as a treat.

– He agreed to play tennis the next day.

Check that you have used all the punctuation needed.

 The accuracy of what you say when using indirect speech depends mainly on the situation. For example, if you were telling a friend about the details of a bullying incident you had seen, you might only include the basic points. Whereas, if you were reporting the incident to your teacher, your account would need to be as accurate as possible.

Imagine this situation:
You are worried about your friend, Gina. She has been crying in the classroom, during break and has told you why.

Make a list of the main points you are going to include, then write two paragraphs involving indirect speech; one in which you tell your sister about Gina, the other in which you tell your teacher.

Further work and revision

 You are a BBC reporter at the scene of a big news event. You are interviewing a member of the public and also commenting on what others have said. Write the news story using direct and indirect speech.
Begin with an opening paragraph such as this:

I arrived with the camera crew around 4am to find ...

 Write two sentences about the difficulties of mending an old bike.
One sentence should contain a colon; the other a semicolon.

Tests

The following exercises will help test what you have learned in Section 3.

 Write out these sentences, underlining the subject, circling the verb and ticking the object.

- He banged the drum.
- The dancers spun across the floor.
- The audience clapped their hands.

 Write out these sentences. Underline the main clause and circle the subordinate clause.

- The pond froze as the temperature began to drop.
- The car, which had run out of petrol, stopped.
- If you need help you must ask me.

 Write sentences using each of the following connectives:

soon afterwards
instead
as a result
because

 These connectives don't make sense.
Copy the passage out and replace them with better ones.

After he dived into the pool he put his swimming-costume on, which made everyone laugh as it was bright pink with white spots. Much later as he surfaced, he realised his error, got out and went and changed. He explained that it was because he'd forgotten his contact lenses. Lastly he'd left them on the train, and firstly he'd lost his spare set too. In the same way, the following week he remembered his latest set of lenses and no problems occurred.

 Copy and complete the following table with comparatives and superlatives. Two have been done for you.

	Comparative	Superlative
smart		
greedy		greediest
happy	happier	
anxious		
easily		

Punctuate the following with colons and semicolons.

- Yesterday I bought apples, mangoes and bananas tomorrow I'll buy some tea.
- She said that the directions were simple first right, first left, then straight ahead.
- Miriam looks after the cat Isaac looks after the dog.

 Join these words correctly.
Some need a hyphen, while others become one word.

road hog
multiple choice
semi detached
sun light
super sonic

How is a hyphen different from a dash?
Write a sentence to explain.

 Punctuate the following using double and single inverted commas. Add any other punctuation you think is necessary.

- They bought the video Seventh Zone from their local shop.
- What was all that noise about he inquired.
- Can you repeat the question? she asked I didn't hear the first time.

 Change the following indirect speech to direct speech.

- She told him to adjust the microscope carefully.
- Mr Jones agreed that Anna could have a job delivering newspapers.
- She wondered if she could look through the telescope at the night sky.

Longer assignments

> *Below are a number of longer assignments based on what you have learned in Section 3. Part One contains two compulsory tasks, Part Two gives you a choice of several assignments.*

Part One: Compulsory

 The following should use **simple** and **complex** sentences, **connectives**, **comparatives** and **superlatives**.

a) You are a reporter for a local paper.

Either:

write an article about the poor performance of the town's football team and what should be done to improve it.

or:

write an article against a plan to build a bypass around the town that will damage the environment.

b) Now write a letter from a reader who does not agree with your article. Give clear reasons why.

 Write a ten-line poem using words that have hyphens.
Your poem does not have to rhyme and can be about a subject of your own choice, or you can choose from the following ideas:

Ideas

– a parachute jump
– jealousy and/or revenge
– a tall story

Useful words

– sky-high
– free-fall
– green-eyed monster
– bitter-sweet
– far-fetched
– make-believe

Use words you know or combine words to suit your subject.

Part Two

Choose two of the following:

 a) Make a list of rules to encourage people to look after their local park, which has: a river, a pond, a wildlife area, an adventure playground for younger children only and several paths.

Use the **colon**, the **semicolon** and the **dash**.

b) Draw a small sketch map of the park which is to be printed on the back of the rules. Label it. Your map should help to make the rules clear, but should not replace them.

 Write a dialogue between a father and his son about playing truant. The boy has been caught and the father is at first angry and then, worried. He tries to find out the reason for the truancy.

Use the **apostrophe** to show shortened words and possession.

 You are stuck in the middle of the Sahara Desert. Your camel, an intelligent creature and usually a friendly one, is refusing to move. There is an oasis (waterhole) a couple of kilometres away.

Write an account (about 150 words) of how you persuade your camel to carry on.

Use **direct** and **indirect** speech.

 You work for Mission Control. A report comes in from an astronaut on a new planet. However, the sound quality is bad, and some words are missing (connectives, mostly). Copy out the report and fill in the gaps.

We disembarked from the craft safely _____ set off. We arrived at a dried-up lake _____ looked fascinating, _____ we took some soil samples. _____ we continued towards a mountain peak in the distance. _____ when we arrived there we discovered it had been a mirage. _____ we were back at the space craft _____ Lieutenant Walters had dropped the soil samples _____ we had to go back to the lake. It was very late when we returned to the craft. It was worth it _____. The soil samples were excellent.

Setting personal targets

 Look through the work you did in Section 3 and make a list of the things you did not understand or did not do very well. Keep your list to refer to.

 Talk to your teacher and choose at least three and no more than five of the following targets. Make sure you choose both reading and writing targets.

Use your list to help you choose.

Simple and complex sentences

- I will vary my writing and use longer as well as shorter sentences.
- I will remember the correct names for clauses.
- When I am using subordinate clauses I will try to make sure that the meaning of my sentences is clear.

Connectives

- I will remember that connectives are used to join sentences or parts of sentences.
- When I am studying books I will try to recognise how writers use connectives.
- When I am writing I will use a range of connectives in my sentences.

The naming of parts

- I will try to remember the names and functions of the main parts of speech: noun, pronoun, verb, adjective, adverb and so on.
- I will try to form comparatives and superlatives from adjectives and adverbs correctly when I want to compare things in my writing.

Using the dash

- When I am studying stories and poems I will try to recognise how the dash is being used.
- I will try to use the dash when I want to make a sharper pause and create emphasis or drama in my writing.

Colons and semicolons

- I will remember to use the terms 'colon' and 'semicolon' correctly.
- I will use the colon when I am making lists, giving examples or explanations.
- I will try to use the semicolon in my writing when I want to show that two ideas or facts are related.
- When I am reading I will try to recognise the different uses of the colon and semicolon.

More naming of parts

● I will try to use the demonstrative when I want to write about the nearness or distance of something.
● When I am writing I will try not to confuse the hyphen with the dash.

Using the apostrophe

● When I am referring to the apostrophe I will use the term correctly.
● I will remember the two different uses of the apostrophe: to shorten words and to show ownership.
● I will use the apostrophe correctly in my writing and not add it to any words that end in 's' (such as plurals) without checking.

Direct speech

● I will use inverted commas when I am writing down the actual words spoken by a character.
● When I am writing I will set out direct speech properly.
● I will try to remember the difference between double and single inverted commas and when they are used.

Indirect speech

● I will remember the difference between direct and indirect speech and use the terms correctly.
● When I am writing I will use indirect speech to convey accurately the meaning of what has been said.

The narrative voice

When we read a story the events are presented to us by the 'voice' of the story or the narrative voice. It can speak directly to us, as in "I saw …" or it can speak about a character as though it were observing or watching as in "He saw …"

If 'I' or 'we' is used it is called writing in the **first person**.
If 'he', 'she', 'it', 'they' or a name is used it is called writing in the **third person**.

Read the following:

a) When Satellite Control called me, I was writing up the day's progress report in the Observation Bubble – the glass-domed office that juts out from the axis of the Space Station like the hubcap of a wheel. It was not really a good place to work, for the view was too overwhelming. Only a few yards away I could see the construction teams performing their slow-motion ballet as they put the station together like a giant jigsaw puzzle. And beyond them, twenty thousand miles below, was the blue-green glory of the full Earth, floating against the ravelled star clouds of the Milky Way.

from *Who's There?* by Arthur C Clarke

b) It was warmer now, as if the ghosts of lost summers had returned to haunt the land. For whole days the temperature rose above freezing, while in many places flowers were breaking through the snow. Whatever was approaching from the north was nearer, and several times a day that enigmatic roar would go thundering over the city, sending the snow sliding upon a thousand roofs. There were strange, grinding undertones that Professor Millward found baffling and even ominous. At times it was almost as if he were listening to the clash of mighty armies, and sometimes a mad but dreadful thought came into his mind and would not be dismissed. Often he would wake in the night and imagine he heard the sound of mountains moving to the sea.

from *The Forgotten Enemy* by Arthur C Clarke

We enter into the feelings and experience of the character whether or not the story is written in the first or third person, but remember that the voice which is telling the story is not necessarily the character.

Try to think of it as the 'voice' behind the words.

Tasks

 Working with a partner, decide whether the **first** or **third** person is being used in (a) and (b) above.

Draw up a table like the following one, and then make notes under each heading.

The Narrative Voice	
Extract (a)	Extract (b)

 2 Continue to work with your partner. Answer the following questions and add your answers to your table:

- Is it the character of the story who is speaking or not? How might this affect the storyline – for example, the ending?
- Does the voice seem nearer or further away from the reader?
- What tense is each passage written in? Explain how changing it might affect the storyline.

 3 Choose one of the titles below. Write one paragraph (the opening one if you wish) in the first person. When you have finished, choose another title and write a paragraph in the third person.

Saturn's Moon   **Dark Days**   **Beyond the Galaxy**
Return   **Seventh Heaven**

Compare your two paragraphs and decide which you like better. If you have time, read your paragraphs to a friend and ask them to say which they prefer.

 4 When writing fiction you can choose to write in the first or third person. This is not always true for other kinds of writing.
A personal letter to a friend must be written in the first person.

Copy out the list below. Decide what person the voice is. Use the following symbols:

fp – first person   **tp** – third person

A biography
A note to a friend
A letter to the bank manager
An autobiography
A sport's report
A diary

Choose three examples from above and write the opening sentences of each one in the first or third person.

Further work

 5 Develop the paragraph you wrote in Task 3 into a science fiction story. Write in the first person or the third person.

Prose and plays

> *Prose is usually taken to mean words arranged in a straightforward way on the page (as in novels). Script differs from prose both in layout and in the way the story is conveyed – through what the characters say.*

Read the following:

Money Matters

Scene 1: A park next to the school. It is a hot summer's day.
Several pupils are sitting around chatting and eating their lunch. Joe is sitting near Kim.

Joe:	I left my money here. Have you seen it?
Kim:	No.
Joe:	Are you sure?
Kim:	Yes ... I'm sure.
Joe:	Where's it gone, then?
Kim:	Don't look at me, I haven't got it.
Joe:	I'm not saying you have.
Kim:	What are you saying, then?
	(Joe doesn't reply)
Kim:	I asked you a question. Well?
Joe:	I'm just saying ... y'know ...
Kim:	*(standing up)* What? What are you saying? If you're saying I've got your poxy money ...!
Ben:	*(Kim's brother)* Are you saying she's nicked it? Are you saying she's nicked your money?
Joe:	Well, no I'm not ... but it was next to her!
	(All three are now squaring up for a fight. Ben pushes Joe. A small crowd gathers.)
Crowd:	Fight! Rumble! Fight! Rumble!
	(Meena, Sue, Errol and their friend Mike are standing by the pond watching. In the distance, Mrs Wetherby, the Deputy Head, is approaching.)

Tasks

 Work with a partner. Note down as many details as you can about the scene above. Include comments on:

- layout and punctuation
- stage directions (the words in italics)
- whether or not it is written in direct or indirect speech
- headings and how the whole play would be organised.

2 Now continue on your own making notes about the following:

- where the scene is set
- when the story is set (in the past, modern-day, in the future)
- when the action takes place (past, present or future)
- what the conflict is
- what you learn about the characters from the dialogue.

 3 Using the notes you have made write three paragraphs explaining how a play differs from prose. (Remember prose can be a simple description as well as a story.)

 4 Change *Money Matters* into prose. You will need to change the stage directions into description and use speech marks and other punctuation. You will also need to use description to convey the feelings expressed through the play's dialogue.

You could begin:

It was a hot July day. The warm air blew fitfully and Kim was enjoying eating her lunch outside when ...

Shaping texts

Further work

 5 Develop *Money Matters* further. Write two more scenes and make a play.
The first new scene should complicate the situation further by including other characters mentioned.
The second (and final) new scene should resolve the situation between the main characters.
Remember to use the appropriate layout and punctuation.

Scripts and screenplays

Plays written for film and television are usually called screenplays, but unlike stage plays they are seen through the eye of the camera. The angle of the camera and the shots taken are essential parts of the story being told.

Here is an example of an opening line from a screenplay:

Opening shot. Wide-angle. Sweep across park showing pupils chatting.

Tasks

 Look at the illustration below. It is a wide-angle picture of the park, at the beginning of *Money Matters* on page 64.

wide-angle

If you haven't already done so, copy out *Money Matters* and add notes about which camera shots you would use. Use the examples here to help:

close-up   medium-shot   long-shot

For example:

Kim: What? (close-up of Kim's face)

You may also wish to consider other kinds of angles, such as looking down from a great height.

66   © Folens

2 Now draw three more camera shots from your scene.
Your pictures do not have to be artistic but they should try to show the differences between the types of shot.

Label each picture, saying what type it is and who or what is in it.

3 Imagine your pictures are 'stills' from a film and are to be printed in a magazine.
They will need captions – these are words written underneath.
Captions are short and usually sum up the pictures. Some are light-hearted, others more serious, depending on the subject.
Write captions for your pictures, like the one below:

Kim loses her temper!

4 Imagine *Money Matters* as a scene from a radio play.
Write down how you would convey:

- the park
- a hot summer's day
- pupils sitting around chatting
- the presence of the minor characters (Meena, Sue, Errol, Mike and Mrs Wetherby).

Consider a range of sound effects and remember you can always change or add to the dialogue, although you must keep to the basic storyline.

Further work and revision

5 Write your own film, television or radio script.
Do not have more than two main characters, keep to one setting and confine the action to one act and three scenes.

6 Can you remember what 'onomatopoeia' is?
Write down three examples that would fit into *Money Matters*.

Shaping texts

Diaries, logs and journals

A diary can be a book for keeping appointments in or for planning ahead. It can also be a daily record of events. Written diaries are not always true, however. Sometimes authors use the diary form to write about the life of a character. The diary (whether 'real' or 'made-up') can provide insights into someone's private life. Usually, but not always, these are in chronological order (order of time).

Read the following:

a)
Saturday August 22nd
MOON'S LAST QUARTER

Went to see Rob Roy's grave. Saw it, came back.

Wednesday September 30th

I am glad September is nearly over, it has been nothing but trouble. Blossom gone. Pandora sad. Bert on his last legs. My father still out of work. My mother still besotted with creep Lucas.

From *The Secret Diary of Adrian Mole Aged 13³/₄* by Sue Townsend, 1982.

b)
Monday, 6 March
I like wandering about these lonely, waste and ruined places. There dwells among them a spirit of quiet and gentle melancholy more congenial and akin to my own spirit than full life and gaiety and noise.

Sunday, 3 September
I went to Bettws in light rain and preached extempore on the Good Samaritan from the Gospel for the day. A red cow with a foolish white face came up to the window by the desk and stared in while I was preaching.

From *Kilvert's Diary* by the Rev. Francis Kilvert, 1870–1879.

c)
SATURDAY, 11 JULY 1942

Dearest Kitty,
Father, Mother and Margot still can't get used to the chiming of the Westertoren clock, which tells us the time every quarter of an hour. Not me, I liked it from the start; it sounds so reassuring, especially at night. You no doubt want to hear what I think of being in hiding. Well, all I can say is that I don't really know yet. I don't think I'll ever feel at home in this house, but that doesn't mean I hate it.

COMMENT ADDED BY ANNE ON 28 SEPTEMBER 1942:
Not being able to go outside upsets me more than I can say, and I'm terrified our hiding place will be discovered and that we'll be shot. That, of course, is a fairly dismal prospect.

From *Anne Frank – The Diary of A Young Girl, 1942–1944.*

Tasks

 Copy out the following headings:

Diary extracts a, b, c	
Similarities	Differences

Now, complete the table after you have considered these points:

- the layout
- whether the extracts are written in the first or third person
- whether they are fact or fiction
- who has written them and how they are feeling at the time
- who the extracts are written for (think carefully)
- when they were written.

 2 Write three short paragraphs saying what you can tell about the person in each extract.

 3 A **log** is rather like a diary but it provides facts about a voyage or the history of a car, for example. The term '**journal**', which is used less often today, can be a diary, a daily publication or a report of events. It usually gives an interesting account of the times, the historical period in which it is written, and is often in chronological order.

Decide whether these are chronologies or not. Write down your answers.

- A cookery book.
- An address book.
- A thesaurus.
- Daniel Defoe's *Journal of the Plague Year (1722)*.

- The Oxford English Grammar.
- A ship's log.
- A book of Special Days.

 4 Make your own time line like the one below:

Start with your birth date. Add important events and also times that are special to you (such as when you were given your first pet – if you were!).

Born

 5 Write your own diary over three days. Plan your diary, restricting yourself to no more than ten lines for each day. Choose to write about events you will want to read again. (Remember, you will be the reader as well as the writer.) If you have a boring day, for example, try to record it in a funny way.

Further work

 6 Make up a character who becomes famous for a brief period (they might save someone from drowning, or win the lottery). Write their diary for seven days. Think about the problems as well as the excitement that new-found fame brings.

Questionnaires

> Questionnaires are used to find out information about particular things, so you should be very clear about what you are trying to find out. The kinds of questions are very important. Open questions encourage many different answers, while closed questions encourage only one – or a few.
>
> *For example:*
>
> | | | |
> |---|---|---|
> | What do you think about ... ? | = | open question |
> | How old are you ... ? | = | closed question |

Look at this questionnaire:

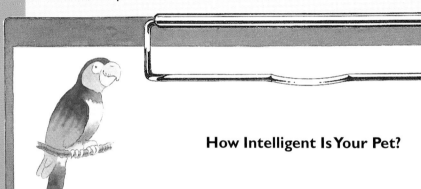

How Intelligent Is Your Pet?

Type of pet _____ Name _____ Age _____

Does your pet:	Never	Sometimes	Often	Always

1. Know you?
2. Greet you when you come home?
3. Ask for food at the same time?
4. Keep itself clean?

Marking key: Never = 0   Sometimes = 1   Often = 2   Always = 3

 Tasks

1 Discuss with a friend:

 – what the questionnaire is trying to find out
 – what you have to do to fill it in (write full answers – or simply use ticks?)
 – how you score it.

What kind of questions are being asked; open or closed?

Copy out the questionnaire and add five more questions. Think carefully about what to ask. Make sure it is clearly presented. Then try it out on some of your friends.

 Decide whether these are **open** or **closed** questions.

- What is your name?
- What do you think he meant?
- What date is your birthday?
- How do you think she would feel about that?
- How old are you?
- What could have happened?

Write down your answers like this:

What is your name?   = closed

 Discuss with a partner the results of your questionnaire.

Consider the following:

- Did your five questions – and the ones already printed – help you find out what you wanted to know?
- Were they open, closed questions or both?
- Was the choice of subject (finding out how intelligent your pet is) a good one or not? Explain your answer.

Draw up a list of any problems you encountered. Think of at least three ways you could improve the questionnaire.

Further work and revision

 Write your own questionnaire about a more serious subject such as blood sports. Try not to make it too complicated.
Remember you do not have to have a marking key. You may only want to find out what people think.
Ask five to ten people and present your findings in an interesting way (for example, as a graph).

 What can you remember about punctuation?
Three different kinds of punctuation are missing from the following sentence:

What kind of person is he, if its not too rude a question she asked.

Write the sentence out correctly.
What kind of question is this (open or closed)?

Headings and subheadings

> Headings and subheadings are often used in business letters, reports, job advertisements and anything where conveying clear information quickly is important.

Read the following incomplete advertisement:

A UNIQUE POST

Are you energetic, independent, carefree? Do you like your own company?
Can you endure high winds and stormy weather?
If you answer yes to all these questions, this job may be for you!

Lighthouse Keeper

The Job
As the last lighthouse keeper in Britain, you will be responsible for controlling the light and managing the lighthouse.

Pay

Conditions
High quality living accommodation, own boat, free fish. Lovely view.

Training

Transport to Mainland

For further information please contact:
The Council,
Seaman's House,
Surf Street,
Ballyseal.

Tasks

 Copy out and complete the three missing sections of the advertisement under the subheadings: Pay, Training, and Transport to Mainland.

2 Write a business letter to Ballyseal Council asking for further information about the post of lighthouse keeper. Set out your letter like this:

Your address
(made-up if you wish)

Date

Who you are writing to and their address.

Dear _____ ,

Heading (the title of the post)

The main part of the letter

Yours sincerely,
Sign your name

 3 Brackets are another way used to separate information in a sentence. If used correctly the flow of the sentence is not disturbed too much. For example:

James Smith (called Jimmy for short) is a young man of great courage.

Some of these sentences need brackets, others don't. Write out correctly those that do.

- The River Severn has its estuary mouth in the Bristol Channel.
- You will need pens, pencils, rubbers and other equipment to complete your project.
- She was absorbed in her computer game and did not hear the scream.
- Bring your £20 deposit part-payment next week for the trip to Paris in July.
- She could only find one book *Romeo and Juliet* of the three she had left in the cupboard.

 4 Write a short letter to Jimmy Smith's parents about his progress and attitude in school. Use subheadings.

 *Further work*

 5 You sell unusual vehicles and are going to place an advertisement in your local newspaper for a tandem (a bicycle made for two people) and a motorbike and side-car. Using headings, subheadings and brackets, write the advertisement. Think about who would be interested in buying the vehicles and write the advertisement with them in mind.

Contents, indexes and reference books

An encyclopedia is a reference book providing information on a range of topics organised in alphabetical order. Knowing how to use reference books is important for good research, but you need to know what to focus on. You can easily become overwhelmed by information. Start with what you know about a topic first, before turning to an encyclopedia. Even an apparently simple topic such as 'The Cat Family' can have many aspects to it.

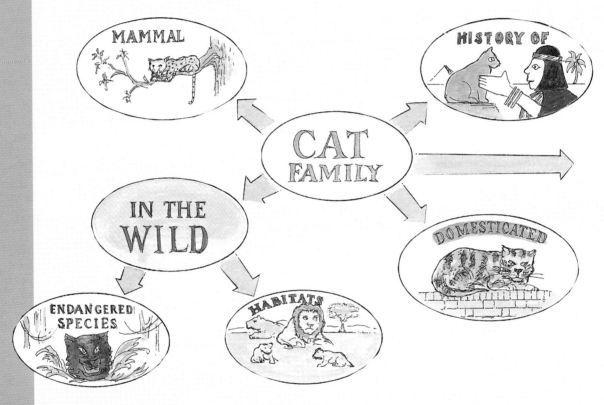

Tasks

 Copy out the spidergram above. Complete it by adding more information of your own. When you have finished, compare it with a partner's. Add his/her ideas to yours.

 Make up your own spidergram on a topic of your own choice or use one of the following:

- sport
- music
- cookery
- school

- computers
- space
- books
- transport

Keep your spidergram. You will need to use it later.

Most books have a contents page, and some have an index. You should be clear about the differences between the two. An encyclopedia has an index but often no contents page. When you want to find out information you consult the index.

Look at the examples below and write down the differences you notice:

The Cat Family	Contents
Cats in the wild	Page 1
Different species	
Habitats	
Endangered species	
Domestic cats	20
?	
?	
The history of the cat	40
?	
?	

Index	Page
care of	18, 25
carnivore	3
deer	10
lion	2, 18
mice	22, 45
RSPCA	30
Siamese	35
tiger	16
vet	33
zoo	16, 18

Copy out the contents page and fill in the gaps using the information from your spidergram in Task 1.

Read the subjects listed in the index. Decide what headings and subheadings they come under in the contents page. Write down your answers.

 Choose one section of the spidergram you made in Task 2. Consult an encyclopedia to find out more. Look in the index first. Use any other reference books you think would be useful. Again, use the index first.
Make notes and write up the information in a simple form for younger children.
Use your own words.

Further work and revision

 Prepare a talk to give to the class or to a group. Choose your own topic. Make a spidergram and research one section only. Write up your notes using headings and subheadings.
Your talk should last two or three minutes.

 Remember the difference between a dictionary and a thesaurus?
Use a dictionary to find out about these words:

gossamer　　　**cochineal**

Use a thesaurus to find out about these words:

obdurate　　　**maverick**

Write down your answers.

Tenses for effect

> *Verb tenses can alter the mood and feeling of writing. We also use certain expressions to help with time, such as:*
>
> *'Yesterday, I lost my poodle.'*

Here are some phrases concerning time:

- A tense is time.

- Time is an elastic band catapulting us into the future.

- History is looking forward to the past.

- Yesterday all my sorrows seemed so far away.

- Tomorrow is just yesterday waiting to happen.

- The moment has gone.

- Now and forever, Amen.

- Live for today.

- The past is another country ...

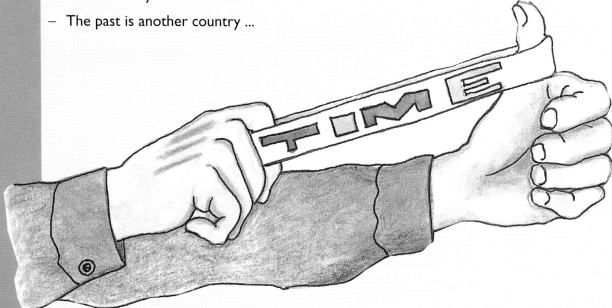

Tasks

 Work with a partner.
Reread the statements carefully and discuss whether they make sense – and if so, what they mean.

 Write down your own definition of a tense, without using a dictionary or thesaurus.

Read this example of a 'time' expression:

<u>Last year</u> I travelled to Africa.

Now write out the following sentences adding the correct words or phrases from the second list.

- We'll be going home.
- He was always the same.
- I will say goodbye.
- She felt unhappy about their talk.

> Tomorrow ...
> Before I go ...
> Afterwards ...
> Whenever I saw him ...

Write three sentences of your own using words or phrases that refer to time. Other tenses can be used to suggest, for example, that an event is possible (**might**, **could**), ought to happen (**should**), or is likely (**will**).

 Work with a partner. Read a) and b) below. Write down the words that have changed. Discuss how this affects the mood and quality of the writing and in particular what impression you have of the character.

a) He looked at his watch. It was eight o'clock. They hadn't contacted him yet. They had forgotten, he thought. They hadn't lied to him had they? As each second passed his anxiety increased and he examined more closely the series of events that had brought him to this moment. Something had happened.

b) He looked at his watch. It was eight o'clock. They should have contacted him by now. They might have forgotten, he thought. They wouldn't lie to him, would they? As each second passed his anxiety increased and he examined more closely the series of events that had brought him to this moment. Something must have happened.

Now write a short paragraph explaining which you think is the most suitable for the content of the passage and why.

Further work

 In 1950 two Danish farmers discovered Tollund Man who was over two thousand years old and from the Iron Age. He had been preserved in peat. Around his neck was a rope. He had been hanged.

Imagine you are looking at Tollund Man in a glass case. Write down your thoughts about him. Ask questions and use tenses such as: 'might', 'must', 'would', 'could' and 'should'.

Connectives across a text

> **Much of our writing depends on connectives because they help us to link ideas. When we are giving explanations and linking events or showing how things are related to each other we need to use connectives.**

Read the following. It is full of connectives.

Hassi-Messaoued

Dear Sir,

By the time I arrived at the house where you sent me to make repairs, the storm had torn a good fifty bricks from the roof. So I set up on the roof of the building a beam and a pulley and I hoisted up a couple of baskets of bricks. When I had finished repairing the building there were a lot of bricks left over since I had brought up more than I needed and also because there were some bad, reject bricks that I still had left to bring down. I hoisted the basket back up again and hitched up the line at the bottom. Then I climbed back up again and filled up the basket with the extra bricks. Then I went down to the bottom and untied the line. Unfortunately, the basket of bricks was much heavier than I was and before I knew what was happening, the basket started to plunge down, lifting me suddenly off the ground. I decided to keep my grip and hang on, realising that to let go would end in disaster – but halfway up I ran into the basket coming down and received a severe blow on the shoulder. I then continued to the top, banging my head against the beam and getting my fingers jammed in the pulley. When the basket hit the ground it burst its bottom, allowing all the bricks to spill out. Since I was now heavier than the basket I started back down again at high speed. Halfway down, I met the basket coming up, and received several severe injuries on my shins. When I hit the ground, I landed on the bricks, getting several more painful cuts and bruises from the sharp edges.

At this moment I must have lost my presence of mind, because I let go of the line. The basket came down again, giving me another heavy blow on the head, and putting me in the hospital. I respectfully request sick leave.

Jean Anselme (translated from the French by Michael Benedikt)

Tasks

 Work with a partner.
List ten connectives in the letter (phrases as well as words). Discuss why they are important and why there are so many.

 Reread the letter carefully and agree between you exactly what happened. Summarise the story in approximately 100 words.

3 Using the notes you have made, draw ten or eleven pictures to show the sequence of events in the story on page 78. You will need to draw the beam and pulley and show the connections between each picture clearly.

4 As you can see, a series of events can also be represented visually. Now look at '**Activities Week**' below. The title describes what happens. It is rather like a logo.

Design your own '**Activities Week**' or, if you prefer, another title related to school such as '**The School Trip**' or '**Sports Day**'.
Make sure the letters represent suitable features and be as imaginative as you can.

Now use your title to write a couple of paragraphs about the event using connectives associated with time, such as:

at the beginning   before   while   afterwards

Make your paragraphs funny and include a particular incident where something goes wrong.

Further work

5 Design your own 'house of the future'. Draw it as a cross-section so that you can see inside. It could be built on another planet, on a space station or underwater. Include a range of household gadgets and robots.

Write a detailed description of it, explaining all the features and how they work. You will need to use connectives.

6 Is the letter on page 78 written in the first or third person?

Putting it all together

> *A good narrative does not have to be very long – but it does need all the right ingredients.*

Read the following. It is an example of a well-constructed piece of writing.

Berlin Wall

1   Darkness had fallen in Berlin and a Siberian coldness was creeping through the night. The square silhouette of the sentry box was barely visible against the moonless sky. For the fifth time in as many minutes Hoffman shivered. It was a lousy life being a soldier, he decided. He would quit the army as soon as his two
5   years were up.
     He looked to his left – most of the lights of East Berlin had long since gone out; and to the right West Berlin was equally dormant. Ahead and beneath was the wall which separated the two. Some said it separated good from bad, freedom from imprisonment. Hoffman sighed heavily. He didn't know – he was no
10   politician. Not like his brother. His brother talked a lot of nonsense about liberation and the like. Hoffman shivered again. At least his brother was in the warm.
     He looked at his watch. Only three hours to go now. Only three hours. Three hours ... Then the alarm sounded, the painful howling telling that someone had
15   crossed the wall and not stopped when challenged. Hoffman stiffened and tightened his hold on his rifle, his eyes peering through the gloom in the manner of the spotlights which were bathing the west side of the wall with intense light. Then they had him. He was a young man and he was running frantically towards a clump of trees. But the spotlights had him and they clung to him. The
20   order was given to fire and the sharp cracks of automatic rifles rang out. Hoffman felt his forefinger curl round the trigger. The man had now jumped on a bicycle and was pedalling furiously into West Berlin. It seemed that he must get away.
     "Shoot, man, shoot!" roared a sergeant from below. Hoffman took aim and
25   tightened his pull on the trigger. The man flung both arms in the air and the bicycle collapsed from underneath him. He was hurled on to the roadway – and then he lay still. Hoffman dropped his gun and found that his hands were shaking and that he had broken out into a cold sweat. He looked again at the fallen body. There was something familiar about its coat. Wasn't it like the one
30   he had given his brother for Christmas? And those shoes with the gold buckles – weren't they the sort his brother wore? Hoffman turned away, his face frozen. Almost absent-mindedly he felt for his gun. Slowly, ever so slowly, he squeezed the trigger again.

Martin Kerry

Tasks

1 In groups, discuss the following and make simple notes. Ensure you understand these basic points before moving to the next question.

Setting, character and plot (storyline):

- where does the story take place?
- who is the main character?
- what is the story about and how does it end?
- who is telling the story?

 2 Characters and plot are closely related. What the characters are like and what they do affects the story, and the story or what happens shapes the characters' outlook. In pairs, write down the answers to the following questions:

- What is Hoffman like? How do we know he is not a complicated person at the beginning of the story?
- How does his character affect the plot? (Think carefully about what happens and why.)
- How is Hoffman changed by his experiences?

 3 On your own, study the way the story is set out and how punctuation is used to create effects. Write out your answers to these questions:

- How many paragraphs are there and when are they introduced?
- How are long and short sentences organised? What effect does this have on the movement of the story? (See lines 13–16.)
- How are phrases used and why? (See lines 11 and 13.)
- Why do you think questions are used in the final paragraph?

 4 Write down your answers to the following:

a) Find descriptions or words that stress the sadness and gloom of the story, such as '**Siberian coldness**' (line 1).

b) What else does '**painful howling**' (line 14) suggest, apart from the '**alarm**'?

c) Contrast the words '**tightened**', '**flung**', '**hurled**' (lines 25–26) with '**frozen**' and '**absentmindedly**' (line 32). How do they stress what is happening in the last paragraph? Find other words that do this.

d) The 'Wall' is a symbol of division and opposition in the story because it divides East from West Berlin. What else does it divide in the story? Think of at least three other things.

e) What is the importance of light and dark in the story?

Further work

 5 Using your notes, write a full essay saying why *Berlin Wall* is successful. Make sure you provide plenty of examples and quotations from the story.

The English language

English is a rich language. Our grammar is based on Old English which comes from the Germanic Anglo-Saxon; other important influences have come from Greek, Latin and French.
Languages change as they are used and English has been enriched by many cultures. This can be seen in some of our everyday vocabulary.

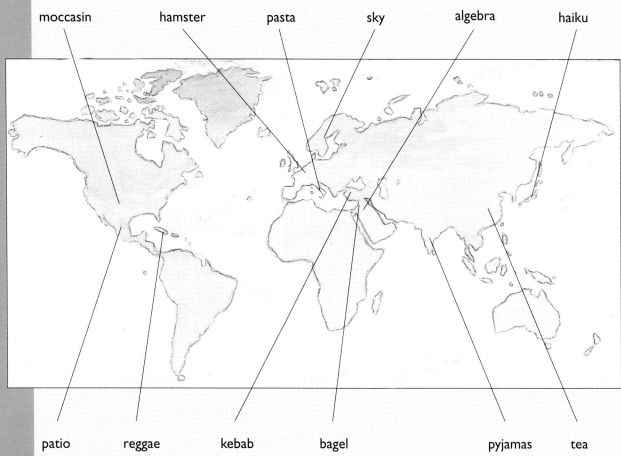

moccasin   hamster   pasta   sky   algebra   haiku

patio   reggae   kebab   bagel   pyjamas   tea

Tasks

 Write down the words labelled on the map, what country (or continent) they come from and what they mean.
Use an atlas and a dictionary to check your answers.

Discuss with a partner why you think English is a rich language. (Think about other cultures and what you know about British history.) Think of at least three points and write down your answer.

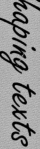

 2 Many of the words we use in English come from (or are derived from) Latin. Write out the following table and complete it like this. (You will need to start by correctly placing the words at the bottom in the 'English word' column.)

Latin (root word)	Meaning	English word	Meaning
centum decem finis manus navis octo plus	a hundred	century	a hundred years

December voice octave final navigate surplus manuscript

 3 We also use phrases in English from other languages to express a particular idea or feeling. These can become changed with use as they fit into the language.

Match the following French phrases to their common meanings.

au revoir
(to re-see)

nom de plume
(name of pen)

enfant terrible
(terrible child)

bon-bon
(good-good)

sang-froid
(cold-blood)

double entendre
(hear double)

billet-doux
(sweet note)

Common meanings

writer's adopted name
sweet
love letter
double meaning
until we meet again/goodbye
coolness in danger or difficulty
someone who behaves in embarrassing ways

Using a dictionary, find out what the following mean:

– à la carte
– joie de vivre
– par excellence
– en route
– beau monde.

Further work

 4 Think of as many words as you can that are part of English and also come from other languages. Choose from your list and any other suitable words on this page and write a 'World Poem'. You could begin:

Tea from China,
Haiku from Japan …

Dialect

> We use the term 'dialect' to mean a local variety of English. Sometimes people confuse dialect with slang. A dialect has its own grammar and vocabulary and is usually pronounced differently.

Read the following:

Plantain and tabouli
Cornmeal pudding
Onion bhajee
Wid plenty cumin,
Breadfruit an coconuts
Molasses tea
Dairy free omelettes
Very chilli
Ginger bread, nut roast
Sorrell, paw paw,
Cocoa an rye toast
I tek dem on tour,
Drinking cool maubi
Meks me feel sweet,
What was dat question now?
What do we eat?

from *Vegan Delight*
by Benjamin Zephaniah

Earwig

The horny goloch is an awesome beast,
Supple and scaly;
It has two horns, and a hantle of feet,
And a forkie tailie.

Traditional Scottish

Tasks

 In pairs, discuss and make notes on the following:

- The poet gives us a list of what you can eat in his country – but is that all he's saying? (Think about the last line as well as the title.)
- Do you agree with the poet? Explain your answer.
- What dialect is it written in? How can you tell?
- List all the foods mentioned. Where do they come from?

 Write a translation of *Earwig*. Try to guess what 'horny goloch', 'hantle' and 'forkie tailie' mean. Why do you think the description 'awesome beast' is used?

3 Grammar as well as vocabulary can change in many dialects.
Working with a partner, write down what these phrases and sentences mean and what dialects you think they might belong to.

- Ah've nowt t'do wi'it.
- I ain't done it.
- Mi na go.
- Well bad, innit?
- Ah dinnae ken.

Underline any words that you don't recognise.
Now underline any grammatical changes you notice, like this:

Can we have <u>us</u> tea?
        (our)

 4 Although English has changed and been enriched by different cultures it is still very similar to the language spoken and written hundreds of years ago. Rewrite this recipe in modern English.

> **SYRUP PRUNES**
> To make Prunes in sirrope: Take Prunes, and put Claret Wine to them, and Sugar, as much as you thinke will make them pleasant, let all these seeth together till yee thinke the Liquor looke like a sirrope, and that your Prunes be well swollen: and so keepe them in a vessell as yee doe greene Ginger.
>
> *The Treasurie of Commodious Conceites and Hidden Secrets* J Partridge. 1573, 1600

 5 Write **one** of the following:

- your own dialect poem (such as a rap)
- a conversation in a dialect you know
- a conversation in a Scots dialect using the phrases and words below.

aboot – about

lassie – girl or young woman

cannae – can't

masel – myself

auld – old

maist – most

bairn – baby

sais – says

tae – to

blether(ing) – talk(ing)

oan – on

wisnae – wasn't

Revision

 6 Note down the kind of rhyme used in *Earwig* on the opposite page. List any other sound patterns you see in the verse.

Codes and pictures

One of the earliest forms of written communication was through pictures. Early people made cave paintings. The Native American tribes used picture writing to communicate and express themselves. Hieroglyphs (pictures or characters standing for words or sounds) were used by the Ancient Egyptians; the Chinese alphabet is also made up of characters.

Picture writing:

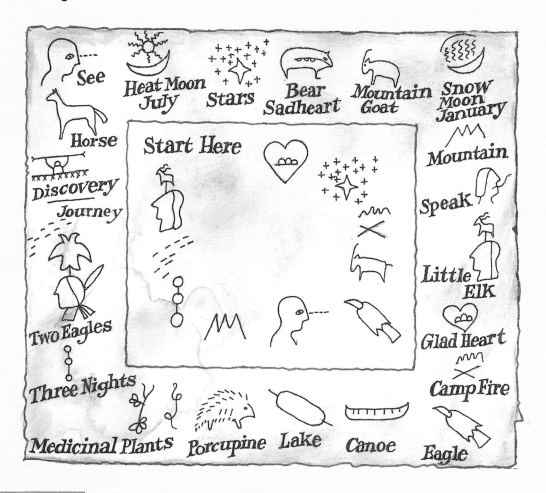

Tasks

 The story above is based on the pictures once used by the Native American tribes such as the Sioux and the Cheyenne.

- Work out the story by referring to the pictures surrounding it. Start in the centre and go in an anti-clockwise direction.
- Now use the pictures – in an order of your own – to make up your own story.

 Make up your own pictures or symbols for words or groups of words. Write a message to a partner and see if they can work it out.

3 Codes can be used to send secret messages.
The code below is based on a number pattern that repeats itself.
Write out the alphabet and finish it.

A	B	C	D	E	F	G	H	I	J	K	L	M	N	O	P	Q	R	S	T	U	V	W	X	Y	Z
2	4	6	8	7	10	12	14	16	13	18	20	22													

 4 Now think of your own pattern (up to M) and ask your partner to finish it.

Other kinds of messages use rhyme and word association as well as pictures.
Can you solve this puzzle and guess the word?

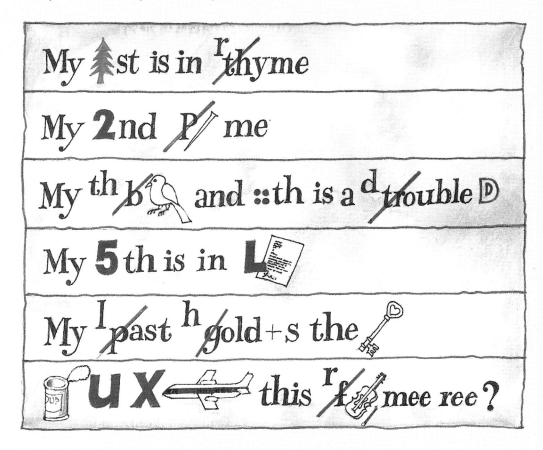

Further work and revision

 5 Draw a map of an imaginary island where treasure is hidden. Add caves, trees and other features. Write three secret messages (in rhyme if you want) that will lead you to the treasure.

6 Write out these words and underline the root.

rotate   **vanish**   **fortified**

What do you think the root word means? Check in a dictionary and write down the language they come from.

Shaping texts

© Folens

87

Specialised language

Specialised and technical language is developed to match new ideas, but new words are often related to much older ones. Some specialised types of language can become part of everyday language, particularly if they are to do with issues that the public is concerned about, such as our environment.

Read the following report.

Scientists and Conservationists Agree

At yesterday's climate conference in Geneva, scientists and conservationists warned that unless world leaders agreed a plan to reduce carbon dioxide emissions into the atmosphere, global warming would continue.

Greenhouse Gases

In today's keynote speech Professor Glenda Wood will explain that global warming occurs when too much carbon dioxide builds up in the atmosphere. She will show how the sun's heat is trapped and the earth's surface becomes very hot like a greenhouse.

Dire Warnings

She will also give a series of dire warnings about other climate concerns. For example, she will talk about how rainforests, which take in a lot of carbon dioxide, are being cut down, how ice in the polar regions is melting, and how permafrost, which keeps the tops of mountains intact, is melting, too. Her colleague, Dr Martin Meadows, will also give a speech outlining how the sea level is rising and how islands and low-lying countries could suffer inundation.

Other issues highlighted by the conference include the way in which deserts are increasing, and how the Northern Hemisphere will have shorter winters. The results of this are that habitats are being lost, and that more and more species face extinction. But it's not just the animals that are under threat; Professor Wood will also speak about the way in which climatic changes will bring more tornadoes.

Tasks

 Working with a partner, write down the words in the report that fit these meanings:

- whirlwind and storm
- natural homes of plants and animals
- a person who looks after the environment
- flooding
- gases and vapours given off or sent out.

Pair these roots to their meanings and note down the words in the report that match.

klima	air
perma	thunder
tonare	coal
hemi	two
di	lasting
carbonem	half
atmos	climate

 2 Decide what the report is about and write down a sentence summing up the main point in each paragraph. (Four sentences in all.)

 3 Each of the specialist words in the columns below fits under one of these headings:

Number   Shape   Measure

List them correctly.

factor	density	polygon
hexagon	capacity	millimetre
octagon	multiple	division
prime	metre	parallelogram
symmetry	volume	cuboid

 4 Many words have common meanings and 'special' meanings.
For example:

face – front of the head with eyes, nose, mouth
            and so on; the surface of a solid

Write down each word and its two meanings.

root	grid
factor	odd
even	counter
chip	

Further work

 5 Create your own science shape-poem like this one here:
Choose a physical process (for example earthquake, flood or tornado) and make a list of relevant words.
Write/draw a science shape-poem, using the best words and presenting them in an interesting way that clearly explains the process.

You might like to consider the following:

earthquake   flood   tornado

Tests

> *The following exercises will test what you have learned in Section 4.*

 1 Write down whether the first or third person is being used in these sentences.

- We were startled by the news.
- I looked out of the window to see the most extraordinary sight.
- I grabbed my jacket and ran downstairs as quickly as I could.
- He walked towards the door, paused for a moment, and left.

 2 Write down whether these are open or closed questions:

- Do you go to school?
- What happened when you discovered that your bike had gone?
- How could you tell that he had forgotten everything?
- How many brothers and sisters have you got?

 3 The brackets in these sentences have been put in the wrong place.
Write them out correctly.

- You will need to bring (scarves, hats), jumpers, an overcoat preferably waterproof and strong boots.
- The holiday the second this year was (a great) success and they were planning yet another one.
- The garden had apple trees, a large lawn recently cut and a small (vegetable patch).

 4 Copy the table and tick the correct boxes. One phrase fits more than one column.

Phrase	Past tense	Present tense	Future tense
I'll			
They had			
Next year she will			
I'm going			
He's tired			

Add three more examples, one for each tense.

5 Write down as many meanings as you can think of for these words:

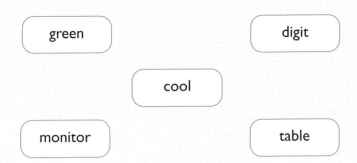

green

digit

cool

monitor

table

 6 Rewrite the passage, which has not been proof-read, using the following connectives to do with time.

- Before I left ...
- sooner than I had expected ...
- while doing ...
- After that I needed to ...

> I rang my friend to explain that I could not stay long because my mother was coming and I would have to collect the children and then make their tea and then do the ironing and then check whether or not my mother's room was clean!

 7 Draw a spidergram for one of these topics:

mammals   **the environment**   **fashion**   **film**   **pets**

Make brief notes saying which section you would focus on for a project and how you would find out information about it.

Below are a number of longer assignments based on what you have learned in Section 4. Part One contains two compulsory tasks. Part Two gives you a choice of several assignments.

Part One: Compulsory

 Use the following phrases to write a prose account about a wild animal. (It should be written from the animal's point of view.)

– no shade at midday
– the fierce heat of the sun
– the search for water
– scavenging for food
– razor teeth
– the dusty path ahead
– the smell of humans
– protecting my young
– the bleached bones of dead animals
– matted fur.

or:

Write a description of a small child who has become separated from his mother. At first he is not frightened because he thinks his mother is nearby. Gradually he becomes more and more anxious.

Write the description from the child's point of view and set it in a crowded street. Conclude your description when his mother finds him. Describe the sense of relief he feels.

 Write a play, script or screenplay involving three characters about a situation in which someone is helped or rescued. Use one of the following situations:

– a market
– the swimming baths
– a theme park
– a riot
– a robbery
– an airport.

Remember to set out your dialogue correctly and if you write a script or screenplay include directions for camera shots in the script.

Part Two

Choose one of the following:

 3 Write a captain's diary of a voyage by ship over four days. Comment on what the passengers are like and what they do.

You should also keep a log about the distance travelled and the speed at which you are travelling.

or:

Write a journal over four days about a particular historical incident you know about. It could be set in the distant past and be about an incident such as The Great Fire of London, or it could be set in recent history and be about a national or international event such as the death of President Kennedy, Marilyn Monroe, Martin Luther King or Princess Diana. Try to capture the feeling of the times if you can.

 4 A farm is to be sold. Use the following information to write a large advertisement emphasising the farm's advantages:

- dairy farm
- good grazing
- set in a valley
- size: 150 hectares
- nearby market town
- new milking parlour
- good rainfall
- large stone farmhouse with modern kitchen
- farmhouse garden with orchard
- hens, ducks and geese
- eggs, yoghurt and other dairy produce
- farm pond
- wildlife and conservation areas.

Set out the advertisement clearly and make it attractive. Use headings, subheadings and brackets.

Give the farm an interesting name, one that suits its location or description.
Give the estate agent a name as well.

Setting personal targets

 Look through the work you did in Section 4 and make a list of the things you did not understand or did not do very well. Keep your list to refer to.

 Talk to your teacher and choose at least three and no more than five of the following targets. Make sure you choose reading and writing targets. Refer to your list in Task 1 to help you.

The narrative voice

- I will remember that the narrative voice is the 'voice' behind the words in a story.
- I will try to recognise the type of narrative voice (usually third or first person) in the stories or novels I read.
- I will practise using the first person as well as the third person when I am writing.

Prose, plays, scripts and screenplays

- I will remember that plays are acted on a stage, while scripts and screenplays are written for the camera.
- I will remember how to set out a dialogue when I am writing plays or scripts.
- I will use the terms prose, play, script and screenplay correctly.

Diaries, logs and journals

- I will remember that a diary is a record of someone's life (or part of it) written in chronological order.
- I will remember that writers sometimes use the diary form to write fiction and will practise using it myself.
- I will remember that a journal is like a diary but also gives an interesting account of the times in which it was written.
- I will remember that a log gives factual information in chronological order about such things as a voyage or a car.

Questionnaires

- I will remember that open questions allow many different answers and closed questions allow only a few.
- I will use open questions when I want to find out how people feel or to gain insights into a situation.
- I will use closed questions when I want to find out specific information.
- I will remember that when I am writing questionnaires I need to be clear about what I am trying to find out and to think carefully about the kinds of questions I ask.

Tenses and connectives

- I will remember the difference between past time, present time and future time and not confuse them when I am writing.
- I will vary my use of tenses to fit the subject of my writing.

- I will try to use connectives such as 'sooner' or 'later than' and other words which refer to time to support my use of tenses.
- When I am writing at length I will try to select my connectives carefully to suit the subject.

Headings, subheadings, brackets, contents and index pages
- I will use headings and subheadings when I need to present factual information clearly.
- I will try to remember that brackets separate extra information in a sentence and will use them correctly.
- I will use contents pages to locate key chapters and sections.
- I will use index pages to find individual items of information in alphabetical order.

Reading and writing stories
- When I am reading and writing stories I will try to notice the relationship between the character and the plot.
- When I am writing stories I will try to use punctuation, such as long and short sentences and paragraphs, to help create atmosphere and variety.
- When I am writing a story I will choose adjectives and adverbs carefully to describe and enhance my story.
- When I am studying stories and novels I will try to notice how the writer has used descriptive language to create atmosphere.

Other languages and dialects
- When I am reading I will try to notice the richness of English and find examples of other languages.
- When I am reading I will try to notice when dialects are used and what effect this has on the story and character.
- When I am writing I will use dialects I know, where appropriate, to fit the characters and make them more interesting for the reader.

Codes and specialised language
- I will try to remember that codes are a kind of language and can be used to communicate information and express feelings.
- I will be aware of scientific, mathematical and technical language and keep a record of words and meanings I am not sure of.
- I will be aware that common words (such as 'face') may have a different meaning in scientific, mathematical and technical language.

Index